Love Tips

Love Tips

Successful Strategies for a Good and Healthy Relationship with Men

Pearly Tan

DoctorZed Publishing
www.doctorzed.com

Copyright © 2017 Pearly Tan

ISBN: 978-0-6482118-8-4 (hc)
ISBN: 978-0-6482118-5-3 (pbk)
ISBN: 978-0-6482118-6-0 (ebk)

This edition 2017 published by DoctorZed Publishing

DoctorZed Publishing books may be ordered through booksellers or by contacting:

DoctorZed Publishing
IDAHO
10 Vista Ave
Skye, South Australia 5072
www.doctorzed.com
orders@doctorzed.com

This book is copyright. Apart from fair dealings for the purposes of private study, research, criticism or review, as permitted under the Copyright Act, no part may be reproduced by any process without written permission from the author or publisher.

The author of this book does not dispense medical advice nor prescribe the use of any technique as a form of treatment for physical or mental problems without the advice of a physician, either directly or indirectly. The intent of the author is only to offer information of a general nature to help you in your quest for meaningful and positive relationships. In the event that you use any of the information in this book for yourself, which is your right, the author and the publisher assume no responsibility for your actions

DoctorZed Publishing rev. date 21/11/2017

Dedication

This book is dedicated to women who are either single or in a relationship looking to better communicate and connect with their men. And for men who want women to understand them better.

"I Hate You And Then I Love You. It's Like I Want To Throw You Off A Cliff Then Rush To The Bottom To Catch You"

– Pearly Tan

Contents

Dedication		v
Acknowledgements		xii
1.	Why Your Man is Tuning Out	1
2.	Understanding Your Male and Female Energy	4
3.	Struggling to find a good man? It may be your mindset	7
4.	Dating Younger Men: Does Age Matter?	10
5.	How to Spot a Player, Not a Stayer	13
6.	Live For The Moment	17
7.	Making Judgements	20
8.	Interdependency or Codependency?	23
9.	Flirting or Hurting?	26
10.	On The Defensive	29
11.	The Laws of Attraction – Unavailable Men	32
12.	Be The Change You Want To See	35
13.	Don't Sweat The Small Stuff	38
14.	Staying Connected	41

15.	Can He Handle Your Success?	44
16.	Enjoying His Achievements	47
17.	Repair or Replace?	50
18.	Keep Calm and Carry On	53
19.	What Do Men Want?	56
20.	Open Relationships	59
21.	Have You Lost That Loving Feeling?	62
22.	Are You Just Using Him?	65
23.	Good Vibrations	68
24.	When Things Don't Work Out How You Wanted	71
25.	Is Your Glass Half Full Or Half Empty?	74
26.	We All Love To Feel Loved	77
27.	Being Present	80
28.	More Than Just A Pretty Face	83
29.	Domestic Violence	86
30.	Fear Of Being Alone	89
31.	A Fine Romance?	92
32.	Rediscovering Your Admiration	95
33.	Love and Religion	98
34.	Hey, Good Lookin!	101
35.	It's Your Move!	104
36.	Resolving Disagreements	107
37.	Two Religions, One Love	110

38.	Three's A Crowd	113
39.	Finding New Love And Losing Old Friends	116
40.	Sharing The Chores	119
41.	The In-Laws	122
42.	Should You Convert To His Religion?	125
43.	What's In A Name – Part One	128
44.	What's In A Name – Part Two	131
45.	Quality Time	134
46.	When Friendships Are Out Of Alignment	137
47.	Respect	140
48.	Unwanted Attention	143
49.	Purely Physical?	146
50.	Separate Bank Accounts	149
	About the Author	153

Acknowledgements

I would like to thank my family especially my parents. Without them, I will not be here today. A special thank you to my man whom I have learned so much about our current relationship and myself. I must admit that I am not the easiest person to live with but with you, I learn to grow spiritually.

There are too many people I want to thank in this book. I strongly believe whoever reads this acknowledgement will know that you are the one that I want to thank for being a part of my life.

I am forever grateful to all these people who continue to make such a big impact in my life.

Thank you! Thank you! Thank you!

1

WHY YOUR MAN IS TUNING OUT

"They could steam up windows with their kisses, but as soon as they started using their mouths for other things—like talking—everything got so complicated."

They say men are from Mars and women are from Venus, and there's nothing like an argument to prove that point!

Have you noticed that men often appear calm and relaxed when women are upset with them? This lack of reaction can seem as though they aren't interested in what you have to say and don't care what you are feeling, but appearances can be deceptive.

Although men may not show their emotions, they can be deeply affected by their partner's distress. It is difficult for a man to see that his partner is unhappy, as he will take the weight of responsibility for her wellbeing and feel that he has failed her.

Men want to be the provider and the protector, keeping their loved ones safe and secure. They are also problem solvers, and this can mean the gap between what you need and what you get becomes a huge source of conflict in your relationship.

If you want to vent your problems to your man, let him know in advance that you only want him to listen, and that you are not looking for him to provide solutions. It will not be easy for him to listen without making suggestions about what you could do to resolve your problems. Although it may feel unnatural to him at first, over time he can learn that listening is one of the ways in which he can support you. Of course, support and understanding goes both ways. It is equally important for you to learn to see things from his perspective.

> *"It is the difference between men and women, not the sameness, that creates the tension and the delight"*

Men often find it difficult to see the value in talking about problems without then talking about solutions. It can seem like a waste of time and energy. Women feel good after talking, as just having someone there to listen is enough. It is one of the key differences between men and women.

By learning to understand one another, your relationship will become much more stable and fulfilling. It is also important to know that your partner will never be able to meet all your needs, and to have unrealistic expectations will lead to both of you feeling bad.

Having a strong support network around you means that you don't have to place all the responsibility for your wellbeing onto your partner. It may be more helpful for you and your partner if you speak to your girlfriends when you have problems that don't need solutions, and talk to your partner when you need advice. It can be a win-win situation for men and women, and one that can lead to greater happiness for both of you. It is an easy way to improve your relationship that you can put into practice straight away.

Understanding one another

Do you often feel frustrated that your partner doesn't seem to listen or care? Have you reached a place in your relationship where you have a healthy understanding of what you can expect from each other?

2

UNDERSTANDING YOUR MALE AND FEMALE ENERGY

"Everything in life is about balance"

Did you know that you have both feminine and masculine energy?

Feminine energy is all about *being* and masculine energy is all about *doing*. We need to tune in to our masculine energy when we want to get things done. The demands of modern life mean that many of us have become so accustomed to using our masculine energy that we have neglected our feminine energy to such an extent it's as though it no longer exists in us.

Do you ever feel like you're so busy running around getting things done that you don't have time to just *be* and *feel*?

It's no wonder we can find it hard to emotionally connect with those around us, particularly our partners, because we are not feeling and connecting to our emotions. This can affect both men and women, and it is completely toxic to relationships.

It is easy, as a woman, to find yourself busy running around doing things for your man, in the belief that the more you do for him, the more he will love you. This is a myth that so many of us have been told, or that we have interpreted from the way we were raised.

Growing up in Malaysia, my parents showed their affection for my brothers and me by doing things for us, making sure that we were clothed, fed, sheltered and provided for. Acts of service were their love language; the way in which they communicated their love for us.

What I have discovered is that the more we do for our men, the more we can grow to resent them, because we feel like we keep on giving without getting much in return. This resentment can grow to the point where we are prepared to walk away from the relationship. We blame the man entirely, without taking any responsibility for our own actions and the choice we have made to do everything for our partner.

"The key to keeping your balance is knowing when you've lost it"

The truth is, we don't always have to *do* to show our affection. Sometimes we can just *be*. When we just take time to *be*, we are calmer, more relaxed and able to be present. In my experience, I've found that men tend to be attracted to women who are comfortable just being themselves.

Your feminine energy is the energy that makes you so alluring and irresistible to men. It is the secret weapon with which you can get men totally hooked. It's like a drug.

Some women choose to focus on their masculine energy and are happy for their men to have a primarily feminine energy. There's nothing wrong with that, if it works for you! I choose to be feminine and I'm very happy for my man to be masculine. My man likes this arrangement too, and so it works for us.

Take some time to think about your relationship and how each of you uses your masculine and feminine energy. Are you in balance? Find the energy that works best for you and your man, and you will find a new level of harmony in your relationship.

Balancing act

Do you and your partner have a good balance in terms of your masculine and feminine energies?

3

STRUGGLING TO FIND A GOOD MAN? IT MAY BE YOUR MINDSET

"We become what we think about – Energy flows where attention goes"

What sort of mindset do you have when it comes to men?

Do you have a mindset of abundance or scarcity? If you have a mindset of abundance then you will always be surrounded by men. You find yourself meeting interesting and eligible men all the time. You can't help but attract their attention and they just seem to keep on coming!

Unfortunately, a lot of single women have a mindset of scarcity. They keep telling themselves repeatedly that all the good men are either taken or gay, and the leftovers are not worth their time.

Does this sound familiar?

I am a strong believer that the universe responds to the energy that you put out. It's a basic law of attraction; if you have an abundance mindset, you will see an abundance of opportunities. If you have a scarcity mindset, the universe is going to keep projecting that image back to you. You are going to continue to find that all the good men are already in a committed relationship with other women (or men!).

"Follow your bliss and the universe will open doors where there were only walls"

I have an abundance mindset. A great example of this is my experience during the period after my marriage ended. Within three months of separating, there were a few men showing interest in me – including my current partner.

In truth, I was happy being single and wasn't looking to begin another relationship, but having a mindset that allowed me to be open to new possibilities and opportunities meant that love came back into my life soon after my marriage ended. My partner and I started our relationship less than six months after my separation and we have been together ever since. I am attracted to my man because he accepts my past and loves me for who I am.

My single girlfriends found it hard to believe that it was so easy for me to find another man so quickly.

They have been searching for Mr Right their entire lives and are still searching. I shared my views about the abundance mindset but they didn't believe me. They justified their position by saying that I'm sociable so it's easier for me to meet men, and they were not open to changing their minds.

It's very hard to help people if they are not willing to be helped. It is like losing weight; many people want to lose weight, but they are not willing to change their diet and lifestyle. We choose how we think about things. We can be optimistic or pessimistic; we can seek abundance or find scarcity. The way you think about things is up to you.

I believe that if you open yourself up to abundance, you will find more of what you're looking for.

Abundance or scarcity – what do you think?

Do you have an abundance or scarcity mindset?

4

DATING YOUNGER MEN: DOES AGE MATTER?

"Age is an issue of mind over matter. If you don't mind, it doesn't matter"

Would you start a relationship with a man who is five years younger than you?

Here's a scenario for you: let's say you are attracted to each other, and although your young admirer is aware of the difference in year between the two of you, for him it doesn't mean anything. For your part, you love being in his company and find him extremely desirable, but you have greater concerns about the age gap and what it might mean in the longer term.

My advice would be that providing you love each other deeply, the age difference shouldn't matter to you.

Age is just a number. The more it bothers you, the harder it is going to be for you to connect with your man, and in the end it could ruin the relationship.

I have a girlfriend who is ten years older than her man, and they have been together for almost fifteen years now. He is still very much in love with her. At the beginning of the relationship his age did bother her. I think it's natural to have some concerns when starting a new relationship when there is an age gap, whether your partner is younger or older. Will you have the same interests? Will their level of maturity match up with yours? Will you want the same things? Will you share the same expectations about settling down, starting a family, travel and work? Will the age difference become a problem for him further down the line?

"It is not our age, but our attitude which makes a difference"

My girlfriend soon came to realise that it would do her no good to carry this heavy, negative energy around with her when she was with her man. All that would happen was that she would push him away, so she decided to live in the moment, and at that point her entire relationship changed for the better.

Some women will worry that a younger man may leave them for a younger woman. However, being with an older man is no guarantee that you will be together for life. That's why it's so important to live in the moment.

Love Tips

Regardless of the age of your partner, you should always be in a position to support yourself financially and be able to move on with your life, should you choose to part ways. A difference in age shouldn't mean one partner leans more heavily on the other. In fact, disparity in age is far less significant than disparity in self-reliance when it comes to determining the success of a relationship. By giving each other the space to grown independently, you have a much greater chance of growing together, too.

Youth or experience – which do you choose?

Would you go out with a younger man or do you prefer older men?

5

HOW TO SPOT A PLAYER, NOT A STAYER

"Beware of the man who is content when his needs are met and yours are not"

Have you ever come across a guy who is physically attracted to you but doesn't want anything more? I'm sure most of us have encountered this sort of man. He's definitely a player and NOT a stayer.

Let me share with you a recent experience of mine. I met a guy in a business networking seminar. He was the CEO of his own plumbing company and his business was doing really well. He gave me his business card and we exchanged phone numbers so that we could catch up for coffee. I was really excited to see on his business card that he was the CEO of his own company, and I was keen to get to know him better.

I wasn't looking for romance; the reason I was excited to meet up with him is because I have investment properties, and it's always good to have a friend in the plumbing industry. As a female property owner, a friend in the industry is a great way to ensure I don't get ripped off if the plumbing at my properties ever needs to be fixed.

Shortly after the networking seminar, we caught up for coffee and then dinner. I was so looking forward to hearing all about how he started his plumbing business, because I would like to start my own business some day and I was interested in hearing about his personal journey to success.

What a disaster!

It quickly became very obvious that I was not going to learn anything about how he started his business. All he was interested in was getting me into bed!

Each time I asked him about how he started his own business, he would change the topic to tell me what an attractive woman I was, how I had such a beautiful body and how he wished he could have a woman like me in his life!

Did I mention he was fully aware that I was in a very happy relationship?

> *"Don't fall for someone if they have no intention of catching you"*

Never mind the fact that I was clearly not interested in pursuing romance with him, the worst part of his behaviour was that he wasn't even remotely interested in anything about me, beyond my physical appearance.

It was all about him. He told me that he had just ended a four-year relationship, and that he was ready for a new relationship but not interested in starting a family, because he already had a 12-year-old daughter.

Believe it or not, he told me all about being intimate with his ex-girlfriend. I was sitting there thinking to myself that he should be keeping this information to himself and not sharing it with a woman he had just met. Let alone a woman who was clearly not single!

Those three hours with him were some of the longest hours of my life!

If you're aware of a man's true intentions, you will choose the right guy to be with. Men are often quite upfront about their intentions. If their intentions don't match up with your own, don't waste your time on them!

I didn't keep in touch with the plumber, but I ran into him on the street the other day and his first question was, "Are you still with your man?" My answer to him was, "YES! I'm still very happy and very attracted to him." His response, "He's one hell of a lucky guy."

I can't say I disagree, I believe we are lucky to have found each other.

> Treat me like a game, and I'll show you how to play!

Now it's your turn to share your stories. Have you encountered a man who is only physically attracted to you? I would love to hear all about it.

6

LIVE FOR THE MOMENT

"Don't wait for the perfect moment, take the moment and make it perfect"

Are you single and longing to have someone in your life? My advice is to enjoy your single status while it lasts! The right man will come into your life; you just have to know what you want and put it out into the universe. It is so important to enjoy each moment and to embrace our lives fully. There will always be times when the grass looks greener on the other side of the fence, whether we are in a relationship or whether we are single.

Of course, the other side of the coin is that it is always fun to fall in love! When you're in love, all you want to do is spend every moment together. You give each other a reason to wake up in the morning, and a reason to stay up late into the night, exploring the beautiful new world that you are creating together, and that is made just for the two of you. Just as you need to make the most of your time when you are single, you need to embrace the moment when you're very much in love, because it will not last forever. Essentially, you should enjoy everything you do and make the most of every moment in life.

"The grass isn't greener on the other side – it's greener where you water it"

There is a story told by my master about two sisters who went to see a psychologist to help them resolve their issues. The older sister was married and the younger sister was single. The older sister was not happy with her husband and the younger sister wanted to get married. The psychologist quickly solved the problem. The younger sister could have the older sister's husband!

You can interpret this in a couple of different ways. It can be seen as an easy and obvious solution to the problems that the two sisters face. Equally, it can be viewed as the psychologist pointing out to them the folly of their ways by wishing for what the other one has. If we spend our time and energy focusing on how green the grass is on the other side of the fence, then it is easy to neglect the grass that we have under our own feet, and our beliefs will become a self-fulfilling prophecy. If we don't care for the things we have then they will not offer the rewards and benefits that they could otherwise bring to our lives.

There may be times in a relationship when you start to doubt if your partner is right for you. You may even start to resent the whole relationship. It's natural to have these kinds of thoughts. One good strategy when you are feeling negative about your relationship is to think of the good times you have shared. In this way you can use your past to improve your present. Now go out there and enjoy the moment, whatever it is and wherever you are!

How green is your grass?

Does the grass always look greener on the other side of the fence or do you feel like you're always standing in a lush summer meadow?

7

MAKING JUDGEMENTS

"The only difference between a flower and a weed is judgement"

Have you ever made judgements about a man before you've even spoken to him? You may have decided that he wasn't worth your time, only to change your mind once you get to know him. Once you discover that he has similar aims and ambitions, that he is motivated, hard-working, with a strong sense of self and a clear vision for what he wants from life, you start to view him in a very different light. Maybe he is running a successful business, investing his hard-earned money in property, and has a great sense of humour. Perhaps he is artistic and creative, devoting much of his time to charity. Whatever it is, once you start to find out more about him, you realise there is a great deal more to him than meets the eye! You might not consider him to be classically good looking, but after spending a few hours in his company you begin to sense there is a strong

emotional connection, and you regret having judged him so quickly.

"Judgements prevent us from seeing the good that lies beyond appearances"

If you have ever found yourself in this position then you are not alone. It takes an average of seven seconds to make a judgement about someone. I have been guilty of this in the past. I once met a guy in a seminar; we chatted briefly during the break and exchanged phone numbers. A few days later we met for coffee and got to know each other on a personal level. We were both already in committed relationships, so the connection we made was not romantic, but we realised we were on a shared path to discover our limitless potential in life, and quickly became good friends.

People will come into your lives in all kinds of situations and circumstances, and the more open you are to the possibility that this may be someone that can bring something positive into your world, the greater the likelihood that you will find the person who you make a deep and lasting emotional connection with. It's all about keeping an open heart and an open mind. It can be easy to close ourselves off from new experiences for a number of reasons, but the wider we open our arms to embrace the world, the more we will be able to receive! It can be very easy to stand in judgement. We are constantly bombarded with images of beautiful people living wonderful lives, but these images have little to do with reality, and they can leave us feeling that there is always something more or something better that we should be striving to achieve. If we focus all our attention on some idealised picture of what life could be, it is easy to miss the beautiful things that do present themselves to us.

Standing in judgement – share your stories

What are your experiences about having judged a man before you've got to know him?

INTERDEPENDENCY OR CODEPENDENCY?

"Today, I will focus on having a good relationship with myself"

Do you have any hobbies or activities that you participate in without your partner?

It's your time to rejuvenate and replenish. I strongly believe that it's a very important component of a healthy relationship. Essentially, it's the foundation of an Interdependent Relationship, where both partners have their own interests and hobbies. For instance, I enjoy Zumba, Hip Hop & Yoga. My man enjoys badminton, squash & tennis. We both make time for our friends, and I love letting my hair down on a girls' nights out just as much as he looks forward to a night out with the boys.

We are two very independent people who choose to be in a relationship. We spend most weekends together; sometimes it will be just the two of us, and sometimes we like to socialise with family & friends, as a couple. Interdependence is a much healthier relationship model than codependence. In an interdependent relationship you are responsible for your own happiness. In a codependent relationship you make the other person responsible for your happiness, or you take responsibility for your partner's wellbeing.

"I used to ask you to bring me flowers – now I plant my own"

When we rely too much on our partner for any aspect of our happiness then the relationship becomes fundamentally unbalanced, and that can lead to all kinds of difficulties for both partners. Sometimes the imbalance can be caused by over-reliance on your partner for financial security, and sometimes the imbalance can be a need for your partner to provide emotional security. It can be easy to fall into these patterns, and it can be hard to break them, but taking responsibility for your own happiness will ensure you have a much stronger and healthier relationship.

There is a wise saying that two trees cannot grow in each other's shade, and this perfectly illustrates the reasons why it is so important to have your own space. By maintaining your own personal space, you can grow strong and truly bloom. If you are trying to grow in each other's shade, then you will only weaken one another, depriving each other of light and nutrition. As much as it is important for you to have the space to grow, you also need to allow your partner the space to grow; otherwise they will never have the opportunity to thrive. It can be easy to become over reliant on your partner, particularly when times are tough, but in the long run it will do neither of you any good. In order for both of you to reach your full potential, you need to be comfortable giving each other some space. In this way, you will both be so much stronger, for yourselves and for each other, and that can only ever be a positive thing for your relationship.

*Interdependence or codependence –
share your experiences*

Which category does your relationship fit into? Interdependency or Codependency? I would love to hear your story. By sharing your experiences you can help and inspire others to make positive changes.

9

FLIRTING OR HURTING?

"Some kisses are given with the eyes"

Do you consider yourself to be the kind of woman who always respects her partner's feelings?

What about in social situations? Do you consider flirting to be something that could be hurtful to your partner or do you see it as just a bit of harmless fun?

When you are in a committed relationship it is normal and healthy to have male friends, just as it is normal and healthy for your partner to have female friends. This isn't about completely cutting ties with the opposite gender. This is about how you interact with other men. They may be single or in committed relationships themselves, but that is not the point. The point is your intentions and expectations. We're not talking about just sharing a private joke or giving someone a compliment on how they look, we're talking about genuine flirting, with the suggestion that there could be more available than

just friendship. If you find that you frequently flirt with other men, it is worth thinking about why you choose to do so. What do you want from them? Do you feel that you need the attention? If so, what does this say about your relationship?

Everyone has different views about what constitutes flirting, but really the defining mark is the intent behind the actions. Some people are naturally very tactile, and some are very gregarious. This doesn't necessarily mean that they are intentionally flirting. Only you can know where the lines lie, but you have to be honest with yourself, because otherwise you are not being fair to anyone.

"Flirting is the promise of more without a guarantee"

Let's turn the tables. How would you feel if your man was constantly flirting with other women? Would you feel respected or humiliated by that sort of behaviour? When you both agree to be in a committed relationship it is important to have clear boundaries, to ensure you do not hurt one another. Flirting may seem like harmless fun, but if you think about what your behaviour looks like from the outside, it is easy to see that it can be very hurtful.

Another point worth considering, beyond the fact that you may be hurting your man, is that you might want to consider how other people may view you if they see you behaving in a very flirtatious manner with other men while you are in a relationship. It is unlikely to inspire feelings of trust and respect from the people around you, if they see you behaving in ways that indicate you cannot be trusted and do not have respect for your partner. It is also diminishing to your partner in terms of how others may view him, let alone how he feels about watching you flirt with someone else.

All of these reasons should be food for thought. What can seem like harmless fun may well have deeper implications that you may not have thought about.

Flirting or hurting – share your stories

What are your experiences? Are you a flirt? How do you handle other women flirting with your man?

10

ON THE DEFENSIVE

"All relationships have one law. Never make the one you love feel alone, especially when you're there"

Do you find yourself getting defensive when your man expresses his thoughts about things you do that bother him?

I used to react very defensively, and in the end it cost me my marriage. If your partner no longer believes he can confide in you without being attacked, then your relationship is not going to work in the long run. If he does not feel safe sharing his inner world with you, where else can he turn? Of course you don't want him to share his deepest thoughts and feelings with another woman. Affairs can easily be triggered by one partner turning to someone else to meet emotional needs which are not being satisfied within their relationship.

If your partner finds himself looking elsewhere for emotional fulfilment, then after a while he may begin to feel he has finally found someone who can listen without judging him, and this may lead him to believe that she understands him more than you do. He and this woman may start to have an emotional connection that feels so good they can no longer resist each other. He will spend more time with her because he feels better about himself whenever he's with her. You will spend more time by yourself at home without him. Anger & frustration will start to build up inside you, becoming more and more difficult to contain, until you eventually explode. Needless to say, that will be the end of your relationship with him.

Even if your man does not turn to another woman for the comfort and solace that he is not getting from you, he is likely to become very unhappy and withdrawn. Try thinking back to when you first fell in love. Would you want to be a source of deep unhappiness in his life? It is easy to shut yourself off from the pain that you are causing to someone else and to only think of your own feelings, but if you want your relationship to work, you need to learn to stand back from yourself a little.

"Wisdom is the reward you get for a lifetime of listening when you would rather have talked"

In order to avoid the sorrows that can grow from shutting someone down every time they try to talk to you about their feelings, you need to become open to recognising their needs. Learn to be aware of your emotions. Be a good listener and allow your man to talk about the things that bother him about you without becoming defensive. You don't have to agree with everything he says, but you do need to respect his views. When he has finished sharing his feelings, thank him for taking the time to talk to you and let him know that you appreciate him. It's that simple. This is something you can put into practice straight away. Give it a try!

Feeling defensive

Do you find yourself becoming defensive when your man tries to talk to you? Are you good at seeing things from his point of view?

11

THE LAWS OF ATTRACTION – UNAVAILABLE MEN

"Don't ruin other people's happiness just because you can't find your own"

Do you realise that other women will also be attracted to your man?

Believe it or not, some women are only drawn to men who are already in a relationship. I call those guys "Unavailable Men (UM)", and the women who desire them "Unavailable Men Lovers" (UMLs)".

The UML may envy you because she feels dissatisfied with her own life, and longs to be in a fulfilling relationship like the one you and your partner have. She will certainly be insecure, but she may not be aware of her insecurities. To her, getting your man may bolster her self-image by making her feel she has 'won' – and if she doesn't succeed, she doesn't need to look at her own shortcomings because she can put everything down to the fact that he was already taken.

"Being the other woman doesn't make you win. It makes you lose... your self-esteem, your values, and your character"

She will be very likely to flirt with your man in social situations, even when you are standing next to him. She will be oblivious to you and your feelings; all that matters to the UML is that your man chooses her over you. Once she's achieved her aim, she may well find that the relationship is not what she had thought it would be, and move on. She will keep chasing other women's happiness rather than making her own.

Why do I say this? While she continues to look for her happiness in a relationship, rather than in herself, she will never find it. She sees your happiness and wants it for herself, but it doesn't work like that. Once she has taken your place in the relationship she will come to realise that she doesn't feel the happiness she saw you experiencing, because the only way you can experience that happiness is if you bring it with you into a relationship in the first place. UML's often fall in and out of love very quickly, because they are continually looking to someone else to provide their happiness.

You will always encounter people in life who have not reached a place where they are able to generate their own happiness. You cannot control other people's lives, you can only take responsibility for your own.

My advice is to be an understanding and supportive partner, and an independent and confident individual. If your partner is satisfied and fulfilled with you, he won't be tempted to look elsewhere. Having hobbies and interests outside your relationship is also really important. Independence and self-reliance are far more attractive than insecurity and clinginess. So be that woman, and no amount of flirting will take your man away from you, that's for sure!

Unavailable Man Lovers

Has your relationship been affected by another woman trying to move in on your man? How did you handle it? Do you think it is better to confront your man or to confront the woman?

12

BE THE CHANGE YOU WANT TO SEE

"You can't criticise unless you participate"

Do you have any girlfriends who have certain expectations of their man?

I'm sure we all do. Let's take one of my girlfriends as an example. She has been in a committed relationship for three years now. One day, while we were catching up over coffee, she told me how her man never bothered dressing up when they went out, and she wasn't very happy about it. I asked her, "What about you? You seem to wear jeans and a T-shirt whenever we meet up. Do you also wear jeans and a T-shirt when you go out with him? She smiled brightly and said, "Yes!" I then asked her why she doesn't wear something nice when she goes out with him. She said she felt more comfortable in jeans and a T-shirt. I'm sure that by now most of you will know where I'm going with this, but she still didn't know what I was getting at. I held her hands and looked her in the eyes and said, "Sweetheart, why do you expect your man to wear something nice when he goes out with you, when you don't put any effort into wearing something nice yourself? What you see in your man is a reflection of you. I'll bet that if you start dressing up when you go out with him, he will notice and start paying more attention to how he dresses, too."

"Your life does not get better by chance, it gets better by change"

Do not try to make a man change into the person you want him to be. Start with yourself. Be the change you want to see in him. It's easier to change yourself than to change others. For those of you who want your man to lose some weight, you can start to go to the gym yourself. Once you have lost some weight and look really good, your man may well start to join you at the gym. He will be inspired by your actions and he will also realise that he has to start making changes in his own life, otherwise he may lose you to someone who is making more of an effort than he is.

It's not playing games; it's knowing what you want for yourself, and being determined to achieve it. Lead by example! Give it a try & let me know how you go with it.

Make the change!

Have you had high expectations of your partner, without being willing to apply the same standards to yourself? Do you think you have a right to an opinion about what your man does, regardless of the choices you make? Do you not really mind about the choices your partner makes, provided you are content with your life?

13

DON'T SWEAT THE SMALL STUFF

"Pride will always be the longest distance between two people"

Have you ever read a brilliant book that you know that your man will enjoy, but when you recommend it to him he shows no interest?

You're not alone. I remember reading a book called "The E-Myth by Michael Gerber". I knew my man would enjoy reading it too, but from past experience I knew that because I had read it first he would not read it. For him, it is a matter of pride. So, rather than recommending the book to him, I simply left it out on the coffee table and went to bed. You guessed it, the next morning I woke up to see the book by his bedside! This is just one example. At times, when I have made a suggestion about a restaurant that I have heard about, he will suggest that we eat somewhere else, but after some time has passed, he'll suggest the restaurant that I recommended a few weeks ago, making it sound like it's his idea. When this happens, I never point it out to him. Instead, I tell him that it sounds fantastic, and I'd love to go!

"Sometimes it's better to react with no reaction"

Occasionally, it doesn't do any harm to stroke a man's ego. I'm sure some of you will not agree with me, and that's ok. Even so, you may consider giving it a try. It can be a very helpful strategy to ensuring you have a harmonious relationship, and I'm sure that is what most of us are looking for.

It can feel as though you are giving a little bit of yourself up by not acknowledging that you had an idea first or that you discovered something before your partner did, but it is worth considering if this is really the case. Does it actually take anything away from you if he thinks he was the one to think of something? And if you point it out to him, how often do you get the reaction that you want? Sometimes it is easier to take the path of least resistance, and to carry your own truths with you, rather than allowing these things to become a source of frustration.

We don't enter into a relationship expecting that it's not going to work one day. Rather than allowing frustrations to build up about things that don't really matter, you can learn to let go and give him what he wants. You may well find that if he feels that you are fully accepting of him, he is able to be a lot more giving in return, and that the things you have been fighting for now just fall into your hands.

Try putting it into practice with your man. I'd love to hear about how it works for you!

A matter of principle?

Have you found that pride has been a source of damage and frustration in your relationship? Do you always stand on principle or do you find it easy to shrug your shoulders and give his ego a little massage?

14

STAYING CONNECTED

"You are a mystery to me, yet so familiar. Like a song I've never heard before, and a tune I've known my entire life"

Do you know why your man chose you?

I'm sure you do! It's because he feels a deeper connection and a stronger attraction to you than he feels for anyone else. There is spark! If a man is attracted to you and you show him you're interested, it won't take long for him to approach you. Finding someone that you really like doesn't happen every day, so be grateful and appreciate every moment you have with him. If you have any obstacles that you need to overcome in your relationship (which is normal for every couple, so don't ever think that you're alone!), you both need to learn to resolve the issues in a mature way.

"Everything is about energy. The way you feel around certain people will tell you if this connection needs to be stopped or not"

Never use the words 'let's break up' or 'let's get divorce' when you're in a heated argument. Always deal with the issue in a calm way. By dealing with your issues and challenges in a calm and mature way, you will build a long lasting relationship. Your man will feel more and more attracted to you each day, unless you have been in a passionless relationship for a very long time and he has already fallen out of love with you. If this is the case, you must make the choice as to whether you want to re-ignite the flamer or move on with your life. Only you and your man can answer this question. If you do both want to find a way back to love and romance then believing that you can do it will go a long way to making it possible!

It may not feel easy at first, but by making a few small changes you will find that you are taking steps to get out of the difficulties that you find yourselves in. Taking a few deep breaths – in with love and out with pain – instead of reacting in a negative way can help to de-escalate situations and give both of you the space that you need to be able to hear and acknowledge each other. After all, this is really what everybody wants in a relationship; to be heard and to be acknowledged. You do not always have to see eye to eye, but you do always need to give each other the respect to listen to one another's point of view, without feeling that the entire relationship is in jeopardy. The only possible outcome of continual threats and fights is that you will grow further and further apart. Focus on the love and on the positives in your relationship, and give your partner the space to express himself, without making him feel the world is going to come to an end. It will benefit both of you, in the long run.

Staying connected

Have you grown apart from your partner? Do you find it difficult to stay calm when you have disagreements and difficulties? Can you remember back to the time when you were first in love? Perhaps you've never lost that connection?

15

CAN HE HANDLE YOUR SUCCESS?

"If you're a strong man, you should not feel threatened by a strong woman"

Do you think that a man will feel threatened by you if you're earning more money than him and have more financial security?

It would probably be true to say that there will be some men who are likely to feel threatened by your success. However, a mature and well-balanced man is attracted to successful women, who are not only financially independent, but are also wise enough with their money to know how to invest it well. A woman like this is sending an indirect signal to men that she knows what she wants in life and that she's a go-getter. Nothing will stop you once you set your mind to it! These personality traits are very attractive to men.

There are many other ways to be independent. Even women who have financial independence may

find that they are emotionally insecure. Emotional independence and self-reliance are also very important to your wellbeing, but as is the case with financial independence, these traits can also feel threatening to some men. We have a long history of women relying on men for their emotional and financial wellbeing, and it has only really begun to change very recently. It can be difficult for some men to know what their role is in a relationship, if they are not expected to be the protector and the provider.

"Most men claim to desire driven, independent and confident women, yet when confronted with such a creature reverence often evolves into resentment"

A man who is committed to a successful woman will up his game in order to be a better man for her. My advice is to be yourself; if your man resents you because you're more successful than him then he's probably not the right man for you. It's not your fault that you've had more material successful than him. If he tries to bring you down to his level so that he can feel good about himself then something is very wrong. Equally, if you are strong and stable emotionally, but he is always trying to find a way to push your buttons or to diminish your emotional health, then this is clearly going to be very damaging to you.

Love Tips

Looking from the outside, it may seem impossible to imagine a string, independent woman allowing such a man to have an impact on her life, but it can easily happen. In the early stages of a relationship it can be all too easy to be influenced by your partner, and if their influence is unhealthy it may take a while for you to notice that you are diminishing yourself in order to please them. Instead of changing who you are to accommodate a man's needs, stay true to yourself. Be the woman that you always wanted to be & NOT the person a man thinks you should be. Always remember that your destiny is in your own hands!

Staying true to yourself

Have you experienced a man trying to devalue your achievements in order to feel better about his own life? What did you do?

16

ENJOYING HIS ACHIEVEMENTS

"Happy people focus on what they have. Unhappy people focus on what's missing"

Are you happy for your man when he achieves his goals or do you get jealous and try to bring him down by criticising him?

If you're happy for your man in all of his achievements, this is a very good indication that you have a strong and stable relationship. However, if you're jealous of his achievements then your relationship is likely to suffer, because your man will start to doubt that you are the right woman for him. He will feel that his best is not good enough, and that he is unable to make you happy.

If you find yourself becoming critical or diminishing him when he has cause to celebrate, it is worth thinking about why. Do you feel his success reflects badly on you? Do you worry that he might outgrow you and want to move on? In other words, is there a reason why you feel threatened by his achievements, rather than embracing them as being positive forces both in his life and in your relationship?

"You can't live a positive life with a negative mind"

His achievements will be devalued if he cannot share them with the woman he loves. Your happiness means the whole world to him, and he will be very affected if you're not happy, even if he doesn't always show it. I remember asking my man how it makes him feel when he sees me happy. His answer was he feels like he has hit the jackpot. It will be the same for your man.

On the flip side, if you continue to dismiss or diminish your man rather than celebrating his achievements with him, he may begin to question whether or not there might be more to life. The fears that you have about being inadequate or getting left behind are much more likely to come to pass if you can't share his happiness.

Rather than seeing his life as a reflection of your own, take a step back and see him as independent from you. By viewing him on his own merits, rather than through the filter of your own life you will be able to see him much more clearly, and it will be far easier for you to give him the support that he deserves and to share the pleasure of his achievements. Start appreciating him and his only desire will be to build his life and his future with you. After all, it is so much more wonderful to be able to share your achievements with someone you love!

Happy together or unhappy together

Do you find it difficult to enjoy your partner's successes? Do you worry that you might get left behind if his life is moving forward and yours is staying in the same place? Do you relish your partner's achievements and encourage him to keep making great strides forwards in his own life, because you believe it will benefit both of you? How do you feel?

17

REPAIR OR REPLACE?

"A relationship is like a house. When a light bulb burns out, you do not go and buy a new house – you fix the light bulb"

My man and I went out to dinner with two other couples. These two couples have been together for most of their lives, and it's amazing to see them still enjoying each other's company. Couple A have been married for 55 years, and they are both in their late 70s. Couple B have been married for 45 years, and they are in their early 70s. Their secret to their long-lasting relationships is respect, appreciation and accepting each other's differences.

One very important thing that I learned from them is that when something is broken, they find ways to mend it. Younger generations are very quick to throw things away when they are broken. It's a wonderful analogy for how we approach relationships. For theses couples, from a generation brought up to find

ways to repair things when they aren't working, if they face difficulties in their relationship they will do everything they can to fix it. In this way, they build a strong and solid foundation. For younger generations, if things don't work out the way we want them to, we will end a relationship without much thought. We take the easy way out, rather than having to face the problem and find a solution to it.

> *"You can't control the wind, but you can adjust your sails"*

The way to learn and grow together is to keep finding solutions to all obstacles in life. By doing so, you will be great partners to each other. Always remember your partner comes into your life to teach you about yourself. If you doubt this, think back to a time when your man said something like, "That dress that you're wearing makes your butt look big." What was your reaction? Were you extremely upset or did you respect his opinion but still choose to wear the dress, because you like it?

If you are continually upset by your partner's comments then you have not mastered yourself yet. If you have mastered yourself, his opinion is just his view and it will not affect your emotions at all. Once again, it's all about respect, appreciation and acceptance of each other. In the end, it's your choice to make or break the relationship. You can keep finding ways to repair the things that don't work or you can take the easy way out and throw it all away.

Disposable or indespensible

Are you inclined to give up on a relationship at the first sign of trouble? Do you believe that if you weather the storms together you will come through as a much stronger couple or do you worry that you'll be investing your time into something that is going nowhere when you could be with someone else with whom you might be more compatible? How do you approach relationships? Disposable or indespensible?

18

KEEP CALM AND CARRY ON

"Anger is fake power. We don't actually control anyone with anger. When we choose to use anger, it ends up controlling us"

Are you the sort of women that find it difficult to control your temper when you're upset about something?

This is something worth addressing. If you are upset and you're not in control of your temper, sooner or later it is very likely to cause your relationship to fail. No one wants to be with someone who is out of control when they're angry. Do you think you would enjoy being with a man who behaved in that way? It's like walking on eggshells. It's okay to feel the anger. This isn't about suppressing your emotions. You can choose to walk away from the situation and deal with it when you're a lot calmer. You tend to find a solution to the problem when you're calmer because you can focus better. Yelling and screaming when you're angry will only make things more complicated.

If you are inclined to unleash a raging torrent of emotion whenever you and your man don't see eye to eye about something, you will very quickly alienate him, and he will either become very withdrawn and reluctant to share his thoughts and feelings with you or he may start fighting fire with fire. Neither of these is a good option, and will only lead to greater unhappiness for both of you. It is under these circumstances that resentments can begin to grow, and that only adds fuel to an already volatile situation. It's time to take a deep breath and think about a different way of approaching things!

> "For every minute you are angry, you lose sixty seconds of happiness"

There will always be a solution to any problem. If there's no solution then there's no problem. It's that simple! A woman who is in control of her temper indirectly sends a powerful message to a man that she's in control of her life. This sort of woman is very attractive to a man. Learn to be more aware of your emotions. By developing strategies that help you stay calm, I guarantee that your life will change for the better, and you will have a much more fulfilling relationship. Simple anger management techniques like giving yourself some time out or focusing on finding a solution rather than focusing on the problem can really help you to stay on control. You may want to consider seeking help if you really feel that you cannot keep your temper under control. Whatever approach you choose, begin making changes today, and you will quickly see the positive changes that happen in your life and your relationship as a result of your efforts. You go girl!

Anger management

Do you find it difficult to control your temper? Do you find yourself seeing red at the first sign of an argument? Have you developed techniques that have helped you to stay calm?

19

WHAT DO MEN WANT?

"When a man truly wants a woman, she becomes his weakness. When a woman truly wants a man, he becomes her strength"

Do Men Want Relationships?

Most men want to be in a relationship and they have a strong desire for their partner to recognise their wonderful qualities. Did you know that 70% of the time, it's women, rather than men, who want to break off relationships or file for divorce? This mind-blowing statistic shows that women are the ones initiating the end of a relationship much more often than men. Does that surprise you? It goes to show that men enjoy being in a committed and loving relationship at least as much as women do!

So, given that men have such a strong desire to be in loving relationships, what are the reasons that they may choose to end things?

> *"What men really want is not knowledge, but certainty"*

If we give a man the impression that there is no way he can please, no matter what he does, or that everything he does is pointless because he can't do anything right, then guess what? He is going to wonder if he's the right partner for us and he's going to begin to doubt whether or not he should even continue the relationship.

If you find yourself being very critical of your partner, it may be worth looking at the reasons why. There is a possibility that he simply isn't the right man for you, in which case the kind and mature thing to do is to let him go, but can this really be true 70% of the time? It might be worth looking at your expectations, and also at your own life. Are your criticisms based on frustrations about what you think he should or shouldn't be doing, and if so, are your expectations fair or justified? Perhaps you are critical of him because it is easier than looking at your own life and addressing your shortcomings? Either way, it's not going to do either of you any good.

You may not be aware that your behaviour can bring about strong emotions in your man, as he may not always show you how he is feeling, but the things that you say and do will have a profound affect on him. Instead of criticising, show your man that you trust him to be a good partner to you, and you will actually inspire him, triggering his devotion and attraction to you. Given the statistics showing the percentage of women who end relationships, it may be as simple as changing your mindset. By thinking of yourself as being in it for the long haul, rather than always having one eye on the door, you may find that your attitude changes and you are willing to work much harder to give your partner the certainty he desires. Be the woman that he wants to be with for the long term by showing him he can trust and rely on your love for him and your commitment to the relationship.

Are you fully committed?

Do you find yourself holding back in relationships? Do you keep your man at arms length by criticising him? Have you thought about why you might behave in these ways?

20

OPEN RELATIONSHIPS

"Polyamory is the desire and practice of having more than one intimate relationship at a time with full knowledge and consent by everyone involved"

One of my girlfriends told me that if she were in a relationship with a man, it would not bother her if he wanted to see another woman. I was shocked to hear that she felt this way, and I asked why she thought it would be ok. Her reason was that men are not born to be with only one woman for a long period of time. It's in their nature to want to be with as many women as possible. She is probably right, to a certain extent. However, I strongly believe that a man can be content in a monogamous relationship, if the woman is truly the one for him.

My personal view is that a man can be with as many women as he wants, but if he choses to commit to me then the relationship will be exclusive. He cannot have me and another woman at the same time. If he has two women in his life at the same time, does it mean that I can have another man as well? It would only be fair, right? I don't think I could do that. My feelings run very deeply, but only in one direction!

> *"Monogamy is desirable for many reasons, especially in creating a stable, emotionally connected home for children. But judging from centuries of human behaviour, it is also a very difficult standard to meet"*

If I found out that my man was seeing another woman while he was in a relationship with me, I would leave him for good. No amount of explanation would make me want to stay with him. He would be making a conscious decision to be with her as well as me, and my view is that I deserve better than that. He could tell me that he has fallen out of love with me instead of cheating on me. If he cheated on me I would feel so humiliated and disrespected.

It is worth noting that my girlfriend who said that she wouldn't mind being in an open relationship has never been in a relationship with a man before! Reality does not always match up with how we picture things, and she may find that her expectations of how it would be to share someone she loved would be very different to how it would actually feel. On the other hand, maybe having an open relationship would work perfectly for her. She is clearly a very independent woman, and perhaps it would suit her needs to be able to retain some of her independence by not committing to an exclusive relationship. We shall have to wait and see!

Share your thoughts on sharing your man!

How would you feel about your man being with another woman while he's in a relationship with you? I would like to hear all about it from your perspective.

21

HAVE YOU LOST THAT LOVING FEELING?

"One of the most difficult parts of life is deciding whether to walk away or try harder"

One of my girlfriends has been in a passionless relationship for many years. Throughout this time she has grown spiritually, while her man is still happy doing the same things he did when they first met. A few years ago she tried to rekindle their marriage, but her man was not willing to do his part. They have two children who are now in their teens, and she is increasingly tired of feeling that she is holding the family together all by herself. She has spoken to her husband a number of times about how unhappy she is, how the relationship isn't working for her, and how she wants to leave. His response is that everything is fine. I believe he is in denial and doesn't want to face facts.

"Being present physically but checked out emotionally isn't a marriage. There is more than one way to leave a spouse."

From the outside looking in, they seem to have it all. They have a big house, nice cars, and two beautiful children. They function perfectly well as a family, but deep inside, the marriage is empty. They fell out of love a long time ago, and the only thing that keeps them together is their children. If you take the kids out of the equation, they do not have anything in common. She has moved into a different place in her life, and her husband has been left behind. They share a home, and a love for their children, but they no longer share interests or dreams for the future. It is sad, and neither of them are willing to let go. It can seem like a very big step into the unknown, which is always a scary thing to do, but although their intentions regarding their children are good, they are staying together for the wrong reasons, because they no longer make one another happy.

Are in a passionless relationship? Do you feel you deserve better? Can you find a way to re-ignite the flame, are you prepared to make the best of what you have, or do you feel that you should let go and move on? Only you have the answer to these questions. If you're in a passionless relationship, sit back and have a think about what you want, and how you would like your life to be. It may help you to see more clearly the direction you want to go in, and the route that you need to take.

Losing the love

What are your feelings? Do you think it is better to keep a marriage together for the sake of the children or do you think it is more important to find personal fulfilment? Would you stay in a relationship with someone if you were no longer in love with them? Do you think that the passion we first feel grows into something else and that companionship is enough?

22

ARE YOU JUST USING HIM?

"People do incredible things for love. Particularly for unrequited love"

Let's say you're not attracted to a man. Would you let him know that you're not interested in him if you knew that he liked you and showed great interest in you? Or would you lead him to believe that he has a chance with you, so you can ask him to fix the tap in the bathroom or change the light bulb for you?

If you have him to help you with these things, then you may save money you would otherwise have to spend on tradesmen, but my advice would be not to tread this path. If you do not like a guy and you know that he likes you very much, it is far kinder to tell him that you only think of him as a friend, and nothing more. Do not lead him to believe that he has a chance if you know you're not interested in a relationship with him. He may feel so rejected that he may find it hard to love again.

Love Tips

"The one who loves the least controls the relationship"

Put yourself in his shoes. If you really liked a guy and he was just using you to do all his household chores, how would you feel? Would you want to be treated that way? If your answer is NO, then maybe it is worth thinking about treating others the way that you would like to be treated. Always remember that we want to love and be loved. So be kind and considerate of other people's feelings, and value them for who they are, not what they can do for you.

It is worth thinking about what it is that you are getting from a relationship where you know the other person is willing to do anything for you, while you don't have any interest in them beyond friendship. Does it make you feel more attractive? Does it boost your ego? Are you scared of being alone, and so it gives you a sense of security to know that there is someone on hand who will drop everything in order to be with you the moment you call? Are you scared to commit to someone you really care about in case you get hurt, and this person is a useful substitute for a relationship where your emotions are on the line?

Whatever the reason, it is never acceptable to use someone. It can be easy to make excuses or to pretend that you aren't aware of the depth of their feelings for you, but if you look to your heart you will know if you are doing something that doesn't feel comfortable. Just because someone is willing to do something for you, it doesn't always make it ok to ask them. By being honest with yourself, you can also be honest with them, and that is really the only way that either of you have a chance of finding happiness with someone who shares your true feelings.

Just good friends

Have you found yourself in a situation where someone wanted more from you than you wanted from them? Do you agree that you shouldn't ask people to do things for you when you know they have their hopes pinned on having a relationship with you or do you feel it's their responsibility to decide where the boundaries lie?

23

GOOD VIBRATIONS

"You attract the energy that you give off. Spread good vibes. Think positively. Enjoy life"

What sort of vibes are you giving out? Positive or negative?

Positive vibes are things like happiness, joy and love. Negative vibes are things like anger, blame and guilt. At times, we carry these negative vibes with us without realising how destructive they are. It is always important to be self-aware.

Take some time to think about what you are projecting, and the feelings that you are holding inside. Do you find that you are often critical of others? Maybe you have a tendency to view things in a rather cynical way? Is your outlook sometimes bleak? Where we focus our energy can have a big impact on how we feel about the world, and how the world feels about us. If we are inclined to only see the bad in things, it can be hard for life to reveal the beauty and the treasures – not because they aren't there, but just because that is not where we have our attention.

"I am not what happened to me. I am who I choose to become"

Are you hoping to meet someone and start a new chapter in your life? If you are giving out negative vibes you will hinder your chances of meeting someone. Work through your negative vibes first. For example, if you're upset because you were cheated on in your last relationship, you have to learn to forgive him before you can move on with your life. What he did to you is very bad, but the damage is done and you are no longer together. Leave the past behind. Forgive him and let him go. Thank him for teaching you a valuable life lesson. Without him, you would not know that you have the strength to overcome something so painful. You can now move on and have an amazing life with another man. The truth is, whatever happened in the past, you've already come through it. By letting go of old pain you can embrace the possibility of new love. You just have to have faith and believe in yourself.

To a large extent, what we project has a direct impact on what we attract. If you are always looking on the dark side of life, the people and things that you will draw to you will be likely to keep you in that negative frame of mind. By giving out positive vibes, you are likely to draw positive people to you, and your life will be far more rewarding!

Meditation and visualisation are two very powerful tools to help change your thinking. Meditation has been shown to help people overcome depression, and visualisation works on a neurological level, to help you make the things you want in your life become realities, rather than just dreams.

Looking on the bright side

Have you found that your thinking has affected your opportunities in life? Have you tried changing your outlook? What were the results? Did your life change for the better?

24

WHEN THINGS DON'T WORK OUT HOW YOU WANTED

"It's sad, but sometimes moving on with the rest of your life starts with goodbye"

A male friend of mine got to know a woman that he really liked, and after going out together on a few dates they started a relationship. I knew that he really wanted to have children, but when he started the relationship with this woman, she was already in her late forties and had two children from a previous relationship. Because he loved her so much, he treated her two daughters as if they were his own, and gave up his dream of ever becoming a father to his own children.

However, after they had been together for a couple of years, things start to go pear shaped. As much as he loved her, he found it really difficult to be with her because she was emotionally unstable and they had too many unresolved issues. She often accused him of not knowing how to be a father to her two daughters and it hurt him badly. All he ever wanted was for her to be happy and to be a good father to her two loving daughters, whom he treated just like his own children.

> "At some point, you have to realise that some people can stay in your heart, but not in your life"

Even though they are no longer together, he is really sad that things didn't work out the way he wanted. In spite of their problems, he was the happiest he'd ever been when he was with her. He was so sure that she was the one for him, and he was planning to build a house so they could start a new life together as a family, so he's had to give up on all his dreams for the future.

Since they separated he has been working all the time, to keep his mind occupied so that he can suppress his feelings of sadness. After all, he has nothing to look forward to when he gets home. He seems a bit lost and does not have much of a purpose in life now.

Losing love is always painful, and it is important to give yourself time to mourn the things you have lost before you move on, otherwise you can carry unresolved emotions into your next relationship. It is equally important to remember that life is change, and that you never know what is waiting for you in the future. Sometimes, we can look back and see that what felt like the most devastating tragedy made the space for something truly beautiful and fulfilling to come into our lives.

As much as he loved his ex and her daughters, I hope that my friend now has the chance to fulfil his dream of becoming a father to his own children. The experience that he already has of parenting her two girls may allow him to step into fatherhood with more confidence and commitment than he would otherwise have had.

Losing love – share your experiences

Have you been through a similar experience, where you've given everything to a relationship that didn't work out?

25

IS YOUR GLASS HALF FULL OR HALF EMPTY?

"Train your mind to see the good in every situation"

A few male friends of mine have got back with the women they broke up when they were young. After almost two decades, they have reunited. It just goes to show that men really want to be in a relationship, even when their hearts have been broken many times. They would rather die trying, knowing that they have given everything they had to the prospect of finding true love, than die not trying at all.

My advice to you if you are single is to remember that there is someone out there waiting for you. You just have to believe in yourself. There are so many available men out there. I found my man just a few months after I broke up with my ex. I didn't jump into a new relationship just because I didn't want to be alone. I'm perfectly fine being by myself, but my belief that the world is full of possibilities meant that I was open to new love coming into my life, and that's exactly what happened. I love him and he loves me too. The rest is history.

> *"Keep your face to the sunshine, and you cannot see a shadow"*

I have met a lot of women who find it hard to change their mindset. It's like looking at a glass; do you see it as half full or half empty? My single girlfriends and I are both looking at the same glass. I look at the glass and see it as being half full, and they look at the glass, and see it as being half empty. Although we are looking at the same thing, we have very different perspectives.

It's all about the mindset of abundance & scarcity. Change the way you look at things, and the things you look at will change. Try not to judge a man the next time he approaches you. By giving him a chance, you open yourself up to new possibilities. You never know, he could be the one for you! When we prejudge anything we close ourselves off from the truth about what it may really mean to us, but because we have decided without finding out, we never get to experience how beautiful and rewarding the experience could have been.

It is easy to close yourself off, and it is something many people do. It can feel safer and as though we are more in control, and although there is always a chance that if you open yourself up to someone they may hurt you, being alone for fear of getting hurt is no way to live.

Try changing your mindset to one of openness and abundance, rather than closing yourself off and not allowing new experiences and opportunities to come into your life. You may find that everything you wanted is right there, ready for the taking! Good luck, and let me know how you go with it.

How does your glass look?

Are you a glass half full kind of girl or do you find it difficult to stay positive? Let me know your thoughts about changing your mindset!

26

WE ALL LOVE TO FEEL LOVED

"Love doesn't make the world go round – Love is what makes the ride worthwhile"

A male friend of mine is lonely, and would really love to find someone special to share his life with. He distracts himself with work, so that he does not have to deal with his feelings of loneliness. I can understand that he wants someone special in his life, so that he has something to look forward to at the end of the day. It would give him an added sense of purpose. Life would be more exciting and meaningful for him.

I'm sure the right woman will come into his life when the time is right. We all want to love and to be loved, and that is just as true for men as it is for women. Men and women may express their feelings differently, but irrespective of gender, everyone is happiest when they feel loved.

Love Tips

"The best feeling in the world is when you look at that special person, and they are already smiling at you"

To a man, a house will feel more like a warm home if he can share it with a woman. If a man was given a choice to be single or in a relationship, I can assure you that most men would choose to be in a relationship with someone they love; someone to share their joys and sorrows; someone with whom they can entwine their hopes and dreams. There is not a man I know who does not view this as his ideal, rather than being single for the rest of his life.

It can sometimes feel as though we will never meet that special someone who makes it all seem worthwhile, but it is important to keep believing that they will come in to your life when the time is right, and until they do it is also important to enjoy the wonderful things about being single. You can still keep building for a bright future, even when you are on your own. In fact, the more energy you put into creating the life you want, the more likely you are to attract the right person into it. If you are focused on realising your own vision for the life you believe in, then you are much more likely to meet someone who shares your vision for what life can be.

The truth is that if you just keep on doing the things that you love, you give yourself the best chance to meet someone who has similar ideas and interests to your own. Not only that, but you will be living a fulfilling and rewarding life, right up to the moment you do meet that special someone. After all, feeling loved should start with our feelings towards ourselves!

Feeling loved – share your thoughts

Do you think we are more likely to find true love when we are able to truly love ourselves?

27

BEING PRESENT

"Be true to life by being true to this moment"

Do you have a man who's physically with you but mentally elsewhere?

Well, I just want you to know that you're not alone. My man is the same! There are occasions when we're spending time together having lunch, and every once in a while he will send a text to one of his friends, without realising that he's ruining our time together. His focus at that time is to resolve an issue with a friend, but to me, he's not present.

When you're present, it's all about the person sitting in front of you. Hence, his behaviour actually ruins our time together, although this isn't his intention, and he is unaware that this is what is happening until I bring it to his attention.

It is so easy to do in this modern world, where we have the technology at our fingertips to stay connected to every aspect of our lives every minute of the day. You only need to look around you, the next time you are out, to see the number of people who are staring at their phones rather than being present in the moment.

> *"Every day, set the simple goal of being more awake and less distracted"*

Switching off your phone still doesn't guarantee that you are switching on to the present moment. It is easy to distract yourself in a million different ways with a million different thoughts or tasks.

I understand that some people can multitask. However, by multitasking, it's difficult to be 100% focused on any of the things that you are doing. In fact, research shows that multitasking doesn't really work and can be bad for your health, because it stresses the mind. What we think of as multitasking is really task-switching, and constantly changing where we have our attention doesn't produce the best results. When it comes to your personal life, in order to maintain a good and healthy relationship both couples have to do their bit, by being 100% focused on each other when they're spending quality time together.

Learning to stay present is a skill, and one that it can take some time to master. Meditation is a very good technique for helping to keep you in the here and now, rather than your thoughts and attention being scattered to the four winds!

Next time you are with your partner make a conscious effort to be present for him, and you may well find that you are rewarded by him returning the favour and focusing his attention on you. Try it, and see if it works!

In the present

Do you find that you are constantly distracted by other things on your life that require your time and attention, so that it is hard for you to stay present? Has this had a negative impact on your relationship? Have you found any techniques that have helped you to be in the moment?

28

MORE THAN JUST A PRETTY FACE

"It's that quality possessed by some that draws all others with a magnetic force. With 'IT' you win all men if you are a woman – and all women if you are a man. 'IT can be a quality of the mind as well as a physical attraction"

Which one of these qualities that you think a man will be attracted to -physical, emotional or intellectual?

I'm sure that most people will say physical. To a certain extent this is the truth, because most men are visual. In this context, I am referring to appearance. When a man sees you for the first time and feels attracted to you, the chances are he would like to get to know you better.

A man will only get to experience the emotional and intellectual attraction that he feels for a woman after he has begun to get to know her. If he develops an emotional and intellectual attraction to her, he is likely to be under her spell forever.

"Love is a journey from the first blush of physical attraction to a marriage of souls"

What do you consider to be your greatest strength when it comes to attracting men? Do you consider yourself able to quickly form a strong emotional connection with the guys you meet? Are you confident in your intellectual abilities, and love to find common ground talking about thoughts and ideas? Perhaps you primarily use your physical attributes to attract men and have found that this is enough to keep them interested? Maybe you use a combination of these qualities to wow your men, or have you found that they quickly back off when they realise you're smarter than they are?

Everyone has different strengths and weaknesses, and although it is easy to be envious of the things that others have, we are all special in our own way. Physical attraction may be an area where you lack confidence, but had you considered that the pretty girl beside you may feel overwhelmed when it comes to talking about subjects that you take in your stride? It is easy to want what we haven't got, and to imagine that life would be easier if we possessed the things that come naturally to others, but by playing to your own strengths, you are much more likely to find the right person for you. We can always work towards self-improvement, but it is equally important not to lose sight of who you are in an attempt to be something that you think will be pleasing to others.

The most important thing is to be yourself. Take pride in your appearance and your abilities, not in comparison to those that other people possess, but because they are the things that are beautiful and unique to you. Physical, emotional and intellectual, wherever your strengths lie, if you can recognise them and let them shine, you will always be attractive to the right people, for the right reasons.

Physical, emotional or intellectual – what works for you?

29

DOMESTIC VIOLENCE

What do you think of men who hit women?

If you're anything like me, you probably believe that a woman shouldn't tolerate any level of domestic violence from a man. A man shouldn't hit a woman no matter what. I believe most people would agree with this.

However, this has to go both ways. Men are also human beings, and even at the height of anger it is not acceptable for a woman to hit a man.

Using violence is never productive. We all have our breaking point, and it is important to recognise where yours is so that you can remove yourself from a situation before a line is crossed. It is equally important for your partner to recognise where their breaking point is.

Women suffer greatly as a consequence of domestic violence, and nothing should diminish this. It is important to know that men can also be victims of domestic violence. There is far less attention given to men who experience domestic violence, and so it is not always as easy to recognise. Victims of domestic violence often experience feelings of guilt and shame, and for men these feelings can be particularly strong, as they can feel they will be perceived as weak if they have suffered at the hands of a woman.

If you find yourself becoming so overwhelmed with anger that you become violent towards your man, it is worth thinking about why you would feel that this is acceptable, if you would not accept a man being violent towards you. Even if a man is physically stronger than you, you still have the power to hurt him. Violence is damaging on many different levels, and even after the bruises have faded the trauma of violence remains, and can cause lasting psychological damage to those who have suffered at the hands of a partner. It can be very scary and confusing for a man to know what to do if he is being attacked. Even by trying to restrain you or defend himself he may fear that he could hurt you, and that has far reaching implications.

Recognising that violence is never acceptable is the first step to taking responsibility for your actions. Everyone deserves to be respected and appreciated. A relationship that has any element of violence in it is fundamentally unhealthy, so for men and women experiencing domestic violence my advice is to seek help immediately and to remember that it is never your fault. Ever. There are people who dedicate their lives to ensuring your safety and wellbeing are restored to you, so even though it may seem scary and even though you may view it as a betrayal of your partner, you need to keep yourself safe, and the betrayal lies firmly in the hands of the person you trusted to honour and protect you. It is of crucial importance that you get the help and support you need to change your circumstances.

Domestic violence

If you are a victim of domestic violence, do not suffer in silence. Reach out and seek help. Always remember, however bad it gets, you are not alone.

30

FEAR OF BEING ALONE

"Fear of being alone is not a good reason to stay"

Do you love your man or are you with him because you don't want to be alone?

There's a big difference between *wanting* to be in a relationship and *having* to be in a relationship. If you are in a relationship just because you don't want to be alone, I can honestly tell you that you're not in the right relationship.

Most people do not want to be alone. We all want to love and be loved by others, because we are social beings. If you take the time to think about what motivates you to be in your relationship, can you honestly look yourself in the mirror when you answer the question about why you are with your partner? Be truthful. If he's not the one for you, tell him. It's not fair for him to be with you if he loves you dearly and you do not share his feelings. He deserves someone better if you're not able to love him back. Cut your losses now and move on with your life.

By staying in a relationship where there is such an imbalance of emotions you are setting yourself and your partner up to have problems not only in this relationship, but also with future partners. Trust will be damaged, and trust is the bedrock of any healthy relationship.

"Love when you're ready, not when you're lonely"

Did you choose to be with someone that you were not in love with in order to protect yourself from getting hurt? It can be scary to open yourself up to love, but as they say, 'it is better to have loved and lost than never to have loved at all.' Perhaps there are things about your life that you know you need to change, but by being with someone else, anyone else, you can distract yourself from the things you need to do and the changes you need to make. By avoiding the truth, you will only create bigger problems for yourself further down the line.

Before you look for another man, think about the reasons why you do not want to be alone, and work through these feelings so that they do not dominate your choices. By recognising your fears and letting go of them you can make sure that next time around you are truly in love with a man before you commit to a relationship with him. You can thank me later!

Alone in a relationship

Have you ever chosen to be with someone that you didn't love, rather than being alone? Did you get to the root of why you made such a choice? Did you have the courage to end the relationship and let them go or did they make the decision for themselves? Do you regret the time you spent being with someone you didn't love, and do you regret wasting their time?

31

A FINE ROMANCE?

"Romance is the glamour which turns the dust of everyday life into a golden haze"

Which would you choose – a man who is a high achiever but not very romantic or a man who is a low achiever but very romantic?

Most young girls would probably choose the latter, because romantic guys will sweep you off your feet and make you feel like a princess. Romance is sold as being the ultimate symbol of love and adoration that a man can show us from when we are tiny children – just think of all those fairy tales and movies where the hero wins the girl with his deeply romantic behaviour. It is no surprise that many young women view romance as being one of the most important ways to believe that they are truly loved.

Romance can certainly add a sparkle to any occasion, but it isn't always the most practical way to express your love for someone. There are men who focus on providing stability and security, and although this may not be as glamorous or exciting, it might provide you with more of what you are looking for in the long term.

I would personally pick achievement over romance, which may be partly because I'm a high achiever myself, so I have more in common with guys who have similar goals and ambitions to my own. In my eyes, the guys who shine are the high achievers. I have a lot of respect for their choices; they are full of purpose, with a willingness to learn and grow. It doesn't really bother me if a man is not very romantic, just as long as I love him and he can provide for the family.

"Romance without finance is no good"

For most men, being able to protect and provide for the family is very important. It's hardwired into them. I truly understand that women in a modern society do not need men to provide for them anymore, but many men still like to be able to fulfil this role. Even if you are financially independent, it's still nice to be taken care of, and in truth it is not terribly romantic to always have to pick up the bill. That lovely glow may begin to fade and tarnish if you find yourself going without the stability and security that allow you to relax and enjoy your life.

In the long run, you may find that an unromantic high achiever is able to provide you with far more romance than a romantic low achiever – holidays to exclusive tropical getaways where you can stroll along white sandy beaches, candlelit dinners in high class restaurants, bouquets of exquisite roses, all of these things may be things beyond the reach of the romantic dreamer, but something that your high achieving man is both willing and able to give you.

Romance or finance?

So, would you choose an unromantic high achiever or a romantic low achiever? To make you think a bit harder, I'd like you to picture them as being equally good looking and equally devoted to you!

32

REDISCOVERING YOUR ADMIRATION

"Between flattery and admiration there often flows a river of contempt"

How do you feel about your man – do you admire or despise him?

Look to your heart and be honest. No one else can answer this question for you, only you know how you truly feel. What I do know, though, is that life will be very difficult for both you and your partner if you despise him.

Living with someone when you have no respect for them is very damaging to both people in the relationship. Your partner is the one who will suffer the most, as his self-esteem and self-worth are likely to be badly affected by your negative feelings towards him. It doesn't matter where they spring from; you may consider your view of him to be justified because of past behaviour on his part, but even if he has hurt you deeply, it is up to you to make a choice between forgiving him and letting go of the pain or not forgiving him and letting go of the relationship. To stay with someone whom you have no respect for is not fair on either of you.

> *"No relationship is all sunshine, but two people can share one umbrella and survive the storm together"*

If you feel that the relationship is worth saving, and you want to get over your negative feelings and move forward into a place where you feel love and devotion for your man, think back to a time when you really admired him and felt strongly attracted to him. What are the qualities that you were most drawn to? What changed along the way? Can you trace it to one specific event or was the shift gradual? Let the thoughts come into your mind, but let them go, do not hold onto them. Understanding is important, but if you want to move forward then acceptance and forgiveness are where your focus needs to lie. Close your eyes and visualise the time you were happiest with him, when your admiration and love were at their height. Enjoy that moment and keep that happy image in your mind for as long as you want. Allow the sensations of relaxation and pleasure to fill your body, until you are in a deeply blissful state and cocooned by your love from him. Open yourself up to the memories of all the good times that you have shared and all the acts of love and kindness that he has performed for you, until his love for you is like a waterfall, pouring over you and washing away all your negative feelings. Now open your eyes.

How do you feel now? If you continue to be in a blissful state, you'll draw your man closer to you again and reignite the love.

Change the way you look at your man and the man you look at will change. Try it for yourself today!

33

LOVE AND RELIGION

"Love has no culture, boundaries, race or religion. It is pure and beautiful, like the moon's reflection in a quiet lake"

I'd like to pose a hypothetical question, using the example of two people in a loving relationship, but they each believe in a different religion. For the sake of argument, let's say that the woman is a Buddhist and the man is a Christian. They love each other deeply, respect and embrace each other's religion, and have a very happy marriage. They are informed about each other's religions and have made the choice to accept the different views that their partner holds, without seeing it as a reflection of their own views. How do you think they should raise their children?

"We may have different religions, different languages, different coloured skin, but we all belong to one human race"

I believe that the children should be given the opportunity to explore both religions so that they can make up their own minds about what feels right for them. To take things a step further, I do not believe that parents should impose their religious beliefs onto their children. Even if a couple are united in their religious beliefs, rather than belonging to different faiths, as in the example that I have put forward here, I think that it is important for the child to be raised in an environment that gives them every opportunity to explore and discover the world around them, without being guided in one direction or another. If this approach is taken then as the child grows into adulthood they will be well informed, and able to decide for themselves. If they believe that they're better off without any religion, so be it. Religious belief is very personal, and it is important that children have the freedom to make this choice for themselves.

It is a common mistake for parents to feel that they have some level of ownership over their children, particularly when it comes to their values and beliefs, but this is not the case. Children have rights as individuals. It is the role of the parent to educate and to inform, but children must be allowed the room to grow and flourish in their own unique way, rather than having the views and opinions of their parents imposed on them. By presenting them with a broad and balanced view of the world they have the best chance of finding the things that resonate with them. Even if they are not exactly the things that you would choose for them, in order to be truly happy they must tread their own path.

Love and religion – what are your views?

Do you agree? Should children be raised to make an informed choice about what is right for them in their lives or do you believe that it is the responsibility of the parent to ensure their child grows up with a strong religious belief in the mould that their parents cast for them?

34

HEY, GOOD LOOKIN!

"I think people forget that feeling good is as important as looking good, although a pretty dress never hurt anyone"

Do you think it's ok for a woman to give less time and attention to her appearance once she's in a committed relationship?

For instance, she may have stopped working out and started gaining weight, she may have stopped getting dressed up for nights out and not bothering to do her hair or her make up anymore. She may spend much of her time sitting round the house in her pyjamas or her tracksuit, because she feels comfortable in these cosy clothes. Do you feel that this is ok, because appearances don't really matter, or do you think it's important to keep making the effort, even if you're in a loving relationship?

My personal opinion is that it is important to maintain the same standards you set for yourself before you were in a committed relationship, even after you have settled into a comfortable and loving home life. Not only does it boost your confidence, but looking good also generates high energy. Most people want to be around people with high energy. It's contagious, believe it or not!

Think about how you feel when you are dressed up for a business meeting or a night out, now compare that to how you feel when you are wearing the clothes you use to do the housework or the gardening. This is an extreme example, but it is a useful way to illustrate the point. The clothes you wear really do have an impact on your frame of mind. When you are dressed up you probably feel more confident, more engaged, and ready for anything. When you are wearing your scruffiest clothes you probably wouldn't feel that comfortable standing up in front of a room full of people and giving a presentation or hitting the dance floor in a crowded club! The way we dress can really impact on what we present to the world.

Not only that, but most men are visual, and even if they love you just as much when you've crawled out of bed first thing in the morning as they do when you're dolled up to the nines, it's nice to show your man that you care about your appearance, for his sake and for your own.

"If you look good, you feel good, and if you feel good, you do good"

This doesn't mean you need to get dressed up every day of the week, but you might want to consider taking some time to do yourself up if you're going out with him. I think fundamentally, it's about showing that your time with him is special and valuable, and that you want to make the most of it in every way. It's an attitude, really, and taking care of your appearance can be a reflection of the care you take of your relationship.

Looking good!

Do you agree that the way you dress can have an impact on how you feel? Do you think that keeping up appearances is important even once you are in a committed relationship?

35

IT'S YOUR MOVE!

"Seduction isn't making someone do what they don't want to do; seduction is enticing someone into doing what they secretly want to do already"

What do you think about a woman in a relationship sometimes initiating intimacy?

Is this something you think men enjoy? I believe it's good to stroke a man's ego occasionally, and it truly makes him feel like a man to know that he is attractive to you and that you see him as significant in every aspect of your life.

There may be times when it is difficult for him to approach you for intimacy, especially if he is always the one to initiate it, as he may have concerns that you may not desire him as much as he desires you, and he may fear rejection. Of course, if you have a valid reason to reject his advances every once in a while then that's absolutely fine, but if it happens too often it is likely to damage his pride.

"It's so beautiful when the thirst is mutual"

Therefore, for a woman to take the lead sometimes and initiate intimacy with her man can be very healthy for the relationship. It can be a beautiful way to express your love, show your man how attractive you find him, and it can add another dimension to that part of your life, showing him that he doesn't need to feel that he always has to be the one to approach you, but that you are confident enough with your body and yourself to approach him.

If this is something new to you that you would like to try, it may feel a little intimidating at first. The most important thing to remember is that your partner loves and desires you. Holding this in your head should help you to feel a little more relaxed. Wait for a situation where you are both relaxed – trying to get him into bed when he's trying to head out for a meeting isn't going to work, and equally if he's relaxing and catching up on his favourite show or watching an important sports game on TV then you may find that your advances are rejected or maybe even missed altogether, and neither of those things are going to build your confidence. Try choosing a situation where your focus is already on each other or where there are no external distractions. You could surprise him by offering to join him in the shower on his day off or slide your arms around his waist while you are doing the dishes together and suggest he leaves them until later. You will know the rhythms of your lives together better than anyone, so it shouldn't be too hard for you to find an opportunity, and he is almost certain to be pleasantly surprised by your attention!

Initiating intimacy – how do you feel?

What do you think about this? Do you think that it is healthy for men and women to initiate intimacy or do you like to wait for your man to make the first move?

36

RESOLVING DISAGREEMENTS

"One of the truest signs of maturity is the ability to disagree with someone while still remaining respectful"

When a couple has a disagreement, should they resolve the issue themselves or should they talk about it with their friends, particularly if those friends are of the opposite sex?

My advice would be that it is better to resolve the issue with your partner, rather than sharing your relationship problems with others. By turning to someone outside the relationship rather than addressing things with your partner you may well be opening up a very messy can of worms.

Picture a scenario where you confide in your close male friend that you are having problems with your partner. In the process of supporting you and sympathising with your situation, you may well begin to develop feelings for one another that move beyond friendship. The only possible outcome is that things will become even more complicated than they already were.

Imagine the same situation in reverse, where your partner is turning to one of his female friends for support and advice. I'm sure you can see that there is a great deal of scope for deeper problems than the ones you are already experiencing to quickly develop.

Confiding in a male friend may well highlight all the things that you currently feel are lacking in your relationship. He may make time for you in a way that your partner no longer does, he may listen carefully and respond sympathetically, rather than dismissing or interrupting you. Rather than having someone to turn to who can help you through your difficulties with your partner, you may find that you begin to draw comparisons between your man and your confidant. It is important to remember that the time you are spending with your friend is not necessarily a reflection of what it would be like to actually be in a relationship with him, and so to draw a comparison between the two men is really very unfair.

You do not have to have conversations about bills and mortgages with your friend. You do not have to roll him over in the night to stop him snoring. You do not have to talk about whose turn it is to clean the kitchen bin or why there isn't any juice left in the fridge when you just bought a brand new carton yesterday! All of these everyday niggles and complaints are the reality of living with someone. When you are meeting for coffee and a chat for a couple of hours every few days then of course you are going to see the best of someone, so any comparison you make will be very weighted in favour of your friend, and that it really not going to help your relationship!

> *"The purpose of disagreement is not victory or defeat, it is progress"*

Ultimately, no one will have a greater understanding or awareness of the difficulties you face as a couple than you and your man. The course of true love doesn't always smoothly, and if you find yourselves coming up against obstacles, take this opportunity to reconnect and resolve the issues together, so that you can strengthen your relationship and fall in love with each other again.

Do you agree about disagreements?

Do you think that it is best to keep your relationship difficulties within the relationship or do you find it helpful to confide in someone else, in order to get some perspective? Have you experienced getting too close to someone you looked to for help and advice in times of difficulty?

37

TWO RELIGIONS, ONE LOVE

"It is not our differences that divide us. It is our inability to recognise, accept, and celebrate those differences"

Does it really matter if two people in a relationship believe in different religions?

In my personal view it doesn't matter, as long as they love each other. Religion, like money, is something that people can use for their own ends. If we take a neutral view, we can see that neither religion nor money can be inherently good or evil. It is the way that people choose to use them that gives them the qualities of good or evil.

How we use the things that have value and meaning in our lives, whether those things are spiritual or material, is within own hands. Ideally, we will choose to use the things that are important to us in a thoughtful and caring way, to enhance our lives and the lives of those around us. Religion and money are both very powerful forces, and like any powerful force they can be easily corrupted, and used to fulfil desires and to reinforce thought patterns that are destructive and negative.

If we can understand the value that something holds for us, and also recognise that others may embrace different values, then we open ourselves up to amazing opportunities, where we can acknowledge, respect and celebrate each other's differences, without feeling that it is in any way threatening or diminishing to our own values and beliefs.

"I know there is strength in the differences between us. I know there is comfort where we overlap"

Therefore, I see no reason why it is not possible for two people who have different religious views to have a successful and healthy relationship. If the love is there, it will provide the bond that allows them to respect each other's differences and embrace each other's choices. Love is the highest energy that a human can have, and this is, in essence, the heart of all religion. To love and cherish, to respect and nurture, irrespective of the path you take, whether it is Christianity, Hinduism, Islam, Buddhism, Judaism or the Church of the Flying Spaghetti Monster, this is the message of all religion, and the foundation of any successful relationship, so if you take an overview, no matter which faith you follow, your religion can be a beautiful way to enable you to enhance and embrace your partner, regardless of their beliefs, because by doing so you deepen your connection not only to your partner but also to the tenets of your religion.

Love and religion – how do you see things?

Do you think that it is possible for two people with different religious views to have a successful relationship? Are you in a relationship with someone who has different religious beliefs to yours? Perhaps you do not hold religious beliefs yourself, while your partner is a devout believer. Whatever your experiences are with love and religion, it would be great to hear your views and your stories!

38

THREE'S A CROWD

"Jealousy is when you count someone else's blessings instead of your own"

I have a girlfriend who is in a long-term relationship with a man, but they do not live together. Let's call her Felicia. Felicia has a close female friend. Let's call her Anna. Anna is in her late forties. She had a short-lived relationship with a man when she was in her twenties, but has been single ever since then. Felicia has kept her relationship hidden from Anna in case she is upset by the news that her friend has found someone. The reason for this is that Anna is so terrified of being alone in life that she has invested all her emotional energy into her friendship with Felicia, to the extent that she once threatened to kill any man that Felicia fell in love with. It is not born of sexual jealousy, Anna is not a lesbian; she just cannot contemplate the idea that she might have to share her friend or, worse, lose her altogether.

Love Tips

"Blowing out someone else's candle doesn't make yours shine any brighter"

I do wonder if part of Anna's jealousy is the idea that Felicia might find happiness in a relationship, and that she will never have that opportunity herself. I am sure she would be less vehement about Anna being in a relationship if she had found someone to share her life with.

Perhaps is she focused a little more of her attention onto herself, rather than investing all her emotional energy in her friendship with Felicia, she may find what she is looking for. It is very easy to distract ourselves with other people, rather than focusing on our own lives and the things that we could do to change and improve our circumstances, and fear is often the underlying reason why people behave in this way. It often feels easier to focus attention on someone else, whether that is in a negative or a positive way, rather than addressing issues that may be uncomfortable and painful for us to confront in our own lives.

Fear is never a good foundation for any decision we make, but it is all too often at the heart of many people's choices. By allowing her fear to be her driving force, Anna has pushed her friend into a situation where she feels unable to share with her in an honest and open way. This is very sad, as Felicia's feelings of love for her partner are something that she should be able to celebrate with her friend, rather than something she feels she needs to keep hidden.

Friendships and relationships – what are your experiences?

Have you ever experienced a friendship that has become a replacement for a relationship with a man? Would you keep a relationship secret in order to save a friend's feelings if they were unable to find love? Do you agree that some people distract themselves with other people's lives rather than facing up to hard truths about themselves?

39

FINDING NEW LOVE AND LOSING OLD FRIENDS

"The earlier you learn that you should focus on what you have and not obsess about what you don't have, the happier you will be"

I had quite a close friendship with one of my girlfriends before I met my man. However, once I committed to my relationship with him she started behaving strangely. She has never been in a relationship herself, and I suspect that she has strong feelings for my partner, and that because of this she has started avoiding me. It is either for this reason or because she is envious of the happiness that I have found.

I am hurt that she rejected our friendship because of my new relationship. It is hard for me to understand why she wouldn't be happy for me, when she can see how fulfilling my relationship is. I do understand that if she has developed feelings

for him it may be difficult for her to be around me, but I would have hoped that whatever the reason, our friendship would be strong enough for her to find a way to overcome these problems. I would be more than willing to speak to her about her feelings, and it saddens me that she is unable to trust that I would be understanding and supportive, whatever the reasons she finds it difficult to adjust to my new circumstances.

> "Someone else's victory is not your defeat"

The truth is, though, that she needs to be the one to reach out to me. By pushing her to talk when she is not ready, I am likely to alienate her and drive her further away. I may even possibly make her feel justified in her resentment of me, and if that happens then there will be little opportunity for her to work through her feelings and come to a place where she is able to resolve them for herself and move on. All that will happen is she will create a picture where I am at fault and she will be unlikely to think any more deeply about the matter. Therefore, I am focusing on the friendships that I have, and choosing to let her go, for now at least. I hope that, given time, she will be able to resolve her feelings and find a way to be happy for me without seeing it as a reflection of her.

Friendships and relationships – what are your experiences?

Have you ever had a friendship affected by a new relationship? Do you think it is better to hold on to a friendship even when you can see that the person is not happy about the choices and changes you have made in your life or do you think it's better to let them go and move on? Have you found it difficult when a close friend becomes involved with someone new, and did you manage to resolve your feelings or did you lose the friendship as a result of their newfound love?

40

SHARING THE CHORES

"The ordinary acts we practice every day at home are of more importance to the soul than their simplicity might suggest"

If a couple are living together as though they were married, both working full time and with no children to take care of, should they share the household chores? My answer to that question is YES, because they are both working full time, and so there is no reason why one person in the relationship should take more responsibility for the housework than the other.

For example, if one person cooks, the other could wash up. If one person does the laundry, the other could do the ironing. There are even things that it is fun to do together, such as gardening.

The Australian 2016 census revealed that women spend between five and fourteen hours a week carrying out unpaid domestic housework. By comparison, the average Australian man spends less than five hours a week on unpaid housework, so there is still a long way to go until there is true equality in this area!

This imbalance can easily bleed into many other areas of life, leaving women feeling more stressed, and giving them far fewer hours to pursue hobbies and activities that can enhance and fulfil them in ways that are likely to increase their personal happiness, which can only ever be a good thing for a relationship. Our satisfaction with ourselves as individuals has a direct impact on our relationship – the more satisfied we are with our lives, the more we have to bring to our relationship, and vice versa. If we feel dissatisfied and depleted, we are unlikely to have much enthusiasm and may even harbour feelings of resentment, if we see our partner reaping rewards that we can't enjoy, because we are consumed with carrying out menial tasks that take up both our time and our energy. It is true that some people enjoy performing acts of service as a way to express their love, and this is fine, but it should not be to the detriment of the individual. There are many ways that you can show your partner they are special and that you enjoy caring for them without taking primary responsibility for ensuring the space you share is clean and tidy, and that meals are always on

the table for your partner to enjoy. It is good to learn to receive acts of service, as well as to give them, without the guilt that can often accompany having someone do something for you that you feel you should be doing for them.

> *"Sharing makes you bigger than you are. The more you pour out, the more life will be able to pour in"*

In summary, by sharing chores you can strengthen your relationship and grow closer to your partner. It is also a great way to build appreciation and respect for one another. I really enjoy having this arrangement in my relationship. It makes me happy that I do not have all the responsibility for the housework on my shoulders, and that I'm not burning myself out trying to hold down a job and run the house!

Share the chores – share your thoughts

Do you agree that a working couple should share the household chores?

41

THE IN-LAWS

"Family isn't always blood. It's the people in your life who want you in theirs; the ones who accept you for who you are. The ones who would do anything to see you smile and who love you no matter what"

Once a couple have married, and hold the official titles of son-in-law and daughter-in-law, do you think they should treat their parents-in-law as though they were their own parents? Additionally, do you think they should adopt the terms 'mum' and 'dad' when conversing with their parents-in-law, instead of using their names?

In my view, we should treat our parents-in-law just like our own parents. After all, if it wasn't for their love and care in raising the man we have chosen to share our life with, we would not have become part of their family. For me, it is almost symbolic of my gratitude and respect to them for having produced such a wonderful son.

> "Dear parents-in-law, thank you for raising the man of my dreams"

I also like to address them as 'mum' and 'dad' because I feel honoured to be their daughter-in-law and to be a part of their family. It makes me happy to acknowledge my union with their son by using these familiar titles. The same is true when it comes to how my husband refers to my parents. It enhances my feelings of closeness to him to know that he views himself as truly a part of my family.

The blend of formality, by not addressing your partner's parents by their names, but rather giving them an 'official' title, and informality, created by the warm and loving titles 'mum' and 'dad' seems to strike the perfect balance of respect and familiarity; acknowledging their greater age and wisdom, and at the same time creating a bond of closeness and love that recognises their significance in both your life and the life of the man you love. To be able to sum all of these things up in a single word when addressing someone we hold dear is really a wonderful thing, and something that we can embrace wholeheartedly.

It may be worth consulting both your partner and your parents to let them know your thinking and to see how they feel. After all, the idea is to recognise and strengthen a bond, and if for any reason they do not feel comfortable with these monikers then it may be best to explore an alternative or to stick with addressing them in the way that feels most comfortable to them. At least you will have had the opportunity to let them know how much you value them, and by asking for their opinions and views you are showing them that you respect their feelings, as well as holding them in great esteem. They will know they are loved, whatever form of address you all decide on!

Calling your in-laws mum and dad

What is your view on this? How do you address your in-laws? Do you think they should have equal standing to your own parents or should there be a distinction?

42

SHOULD YOU CONVERT TO HIS RELIGION?

"Changing religions is not easy. You may develop some kind of confusion or difficulties"

Does religion really matter when a couple are in love?

I would always choose love over religion. It doesn't matter what religion you believe in. If you love someone, you should be willing to accept them for who they are and not for their religious beliefs. He may believe in Christianity and you may believe in Buddhism. All you have to do is respect each other and embrace each other's differences. Religion should not be a reason that you cannot be together. After all, the foundation of all religion is love and respect, as is the foundation of a healthy relationship, so it should be possible to combine the two!

"Rather than converting people from one organised religion to another organised religion, we should try to convert people from

misery to happiness, from bondage to liberation and from cruelty to compassion"

I strongly believe that if he's the right man for you, he will accept you for who you are and not try to change your beliefs in order for you to be with him. If he wants you to convert to his religion then he may not be the right guy for you. What if you make the decision to convert in order to be with him and then one day the relationship turns sour. What are you going to do? Convert back? What if you do not have genuine faith and belief in his religion, but because you want to be with him you make the decision to convert. I don't think it's a smart way of doing things – you need to be true to yourself.

In order to illustrate this point a little more clearly, let me ask you to think about this: what would you do if you converted from Buddhism to Christianity in order to be with one man, and then if that relationship didn't work out and you met another man that you were attracted to, and he was a Muslim, would you then convert from Christianity to Islam? It is worth thinking about carefully.

Would it have entered your head to convert if you had not met a man from a different faith, and if not, do you think it is right to change your beliefs in order to make your relationship work or do you think your relationship should work regardless of your beliefs?

Converting for love

Can you see yourself changing your beliefs in order to be with a man? Do you think that love comes before religion or do you think that if you truly love each other you should accept one another's beliefs? Would you ask someone to change their faith in order to be with you or would you never consider having a relationship with someone from a different faith because you would fear the expectation that you would have to give up your faith in order to truly embrace their lifestyle and expectations?

43

WHAT'S IN A NAME – PART ONE

"That which we call a rose by any other name would smell as sweet"

I'd like to raise a question with you, using the example of a fictional character called Xena Tanner.

Xena has established herself as a very successful businesswoman over a number of years. She has many contacts and a great reputation. She then meets the love of her life. They have a wonderful and fulfilling relationship, until finally the day comes when he proposes. Xena is thrilled and can't wait to get married, but there's just one small fly in the ointment. What should she do about her surname?

"A good name is more to be desired than great wealth, and to be respected is better than silver and gold"

If she changes her name, she feels that it will almost be as though she is going back to square one with her business. Everyone knows her as Xena Tanner, and her name is definitely part of her brand identity, as well as her personal identity. The logical thing for her to do would be to keep her maiden name in order to maintain her professional profile. In this way, she doesn't have to conduct endless conversations and send out numerous emails explaining the change, something that could be construed as blurring the lines between professional and personal, which may not be something that she would wish to do.

But what if she would really like to enjoy the symbolism of taking her husband's name? Should her professional life outweigh her personal life? For some women it is a mark of love to take the name of their husband. It can be a way of showing your union and announcing to the world that you are joined together with your man by the deepest commitment that can be made.

Perhaps a compromise would be to hyphenate her name, so that she becomes Xena Tanner-Lee. That way, she gets to maintain her professional credentials and can also feel emotionally satisfied through taking her husband's name, which may be a way of having the best of both worlds. It would also require far less explanation as far as colleagues and clients were concerned. It is easy to recognise that the addition of a name indicates a person is married, rather than being unaware that Xena Tanner is the same person as Xena Lee.

I think I would hyphenate my name unofficially, and keep my maiden name on my official documents, such as my passport and bank cards. An alternative would be to have your personal documents, such as your passport and driving licence, in your married or hyphenated name, so that you are 'officially' Mrs Lee, but to continue using your maiden name professionally, on business cards and correspondence, so that you can continue to benefit from the relationship you have worked so hard to establish.

What's in a name?

What would you do if you were Xena? Do you think it is important to take your husband's name or do you think it doesn't matter what you call yourself?

44

WHAT'S IN A NAME – PART TWO

"Names are the sweetest and most important sound in any language"

In Part One of 'What's In A Name' we discussed the options for Xena when it comes to whether or not she should change her surname when she marries.

Let's imagine that Xena chose the option of hyphenating her name, and that after a few years of having a warm and loving marriage, Xena and her husband decide they would like to start a family.

Should their children also use a hyphenated surname, so that they can carry Xena's name as well as her husband's? Or should they just take their father's name?

"Of all the names I've been called, 'mummy' is the best"

I would be happy for my children just to carry their father's surname, because in our Eastern culture, females continue to use their maiden name even after they're married, and their children take on the father's surname, so for me it seems normal and natural that a mother would not have the same surname as her children.

My three brothers and I all have our father's surname, and yet my mother still continues to use her maiden name.

There may be considerations beyond the emotional that have an impact on the decision of whether or not to have the same name as your children. In the first instance, it may give a child a greater sense of belonging and unity if all members of the family share a common name, particularly if this is the norm in the country where they are being raised. It can also simplify things when travelling, particularly if you are travelling without the children's father, as there can be complications at customs if the child does not share the mother's surname. These complications can be remedied with the use of additional documents, namely written permission to travel signed by the father, or a copy of the child's birth certificate and the parents' marriage certificate – it depends on whether or not you mind thinking about extra paperwork when making travel plans, and it also largely depends on the particular customs officer who checks your documents – nine times out of ten they may not question the disparity in your names, but it can feel like an extra thing to think about, and there are more than enough things to think about when travelling with children! It may also simply be more convenient when corresponding with your child's school or identifying yourself in group emails with other parents – once you are someone's parent your identity can somewhat slip into the background, and you find yourself being referenced through them, rather than as an individual!

What's in a name?

What would you do if you were Xena? If you continued to use your maiden name, would you be happy for your child to take on your husband's surname or would you prefer your child to have a hyphenated name?

45

QUALITY TIME

"The most desired gift of love is not diamonds or roses or chocolate. It is focused attention"

Nowadays, people are very busy with their daily lives. However, it is easy to allow this to become an excuse not to connect with your partner when you are in a relationship, and that is a slippery slope that you don't want to find yourself on! It is really important that you make time for each other. In fact, it's a must if you want your relationship to last for a long time. Therefore, it's important to set aside at least one point in the week where the two of you to spend some quality time together.

There are lots of ways that you can ensure you are making time for your partner. In my relationship we have a weekly date night, where we focus on each other and really enjoy spending quality time together. For us, quality time means something along the lines of going out to a restaurant and keeping our mobile phones off the table. No messaging, no texting, no checking emails. All the focus is on the person right in front of you.

Many people, even when they go out with their loved one, are physically present, but their minds are somewhere else. They allow themselves to be distracted by their phone or by thoughts, either running through the events of the day or thinking about things that they need to do tomorrow.

> *"Spend time with those you love. One of these days you will say either, "I wish I had" or "I'm glad I did"*

One day when I was out for lunch with my husband, and he was repeatedly reaching for his phone to send texts and check messages, I gently pointed out to him that he could wait until we got home to respond, and that sharing lunch was our quality time together.

Unless your partner is a doctor or a fireman and it's a matter of life or death there is no reason why he cannot set aside his business to make time for you.

Once I had pointed out what he was doing my partner started to realise that it wasn't good for our relationship, and he no longer texts when we are out together, so that we can take the time to connect with each other, as we are both very busy so much of the time that these moments together are precious. Set time aside and take the opportunity to stay connected, so that you continue to grow together, rather than finding yourselves drifting apart.

Time together

Do you find that you are easily distracted by the demands of life? Are you frustrated that your partner never seems to be able to focus on you when you are alone together? Have you found ways of ensuring you have quality time with your partner, without the pressures of the day crowding in on you?

46

WHEN FRIENDSHIPS ARE OUT OF ALIGNMENT

"Sometimes we expect more from others because we would be willing to do that much for them"

I'd like to put forward a question about two couples with an imbalance in their friendship.

Couple A both have good jobs and invest their money wisely.

Couple B both have good jobs but spend as they earn.

Over time, Couple A have been able to reap the rewards of their investments. They have a great lifestyle; they enjoy travelling overseas, they regularly dine out and they drive a luxury car.

Meanwhile, Couple B are still living hand to mouth. As their responsibilities have grown, their money has had to go further. As a result of this they don't often get to treat themselves. They don't travel much, they hardly ever eat out, and they are driving a second hand car.

Couple A are generous with their money and regularly invite Couple B to dine out with them, at the expense of Couple A, in order to enable Couple B to enjoy fine dining once a while.

However, although they are always very grateful, there are hints that Couple B are envious of the wealth and lifestyle that Couple A enjoy.

My question is this: do you think it would be better for Couple A to find alternative ways of spending time with their friends that don't highlight the imbalance between their lifestyles or should they just accept that Couple B are a little envious of their position and continue to treat them to luxuries that they couldn't otherwise afford?

"When we stop opposing reality, action becomes simple, fluid, kind and fearless"

It can be difficult when you have long term friendships with people and your lives have moved in different directions. It can be easy to start looking critically at each other's lives when you have made different choices, especially if there is an imbalance in wealth or happiness.

Striking a balance in friendships where there is a clear gap in wealth is not always straightforward.

By offering too much, it can be easy for the couple with less to feel not only envious, but also beholden or reliant, and none of these things is ever going to be beneficial to a friendship. It can also leaving the couple with more feeling taken for granted, guilty or possibly even used. On both sides, this can ultimately lead to feelings of defensiveness and resentment, and then things really begin to break down.

Out of alignment or just out of line?

Have you had friendships where you've been aware of growing resentment due to an imbalance in wealth or happiness? Do you think it is better to let go, to address the issues or to say nothing and accept the imbalance? Have you been on either side of an imbalanced friendship and how did it feel? Did you find a resolution or did you sacrifice the friendship?

47

RESPECT

"Love is not a reason to tolerate disrespect"

Do you think it's important to appreciate and respect your man?

My answer is YES! He wants to be your hero and your protector. Most men are hardwired to protect and provide for their loved ones. There will always be exceptions to the rule. There are men who behave disrespectfully to their partners, by lying, cheating or being in any way abusive. These men may well have underlying insecurities and histories of abuse themselves. This is in no way to excuse their behaviour. It is never acceptable to treat your partner disrespectfully, and it would be better for everyone concerned if these men addressed their insecurities without imposing their bad choices and destructive behaviour on anyone else.

It is good to bear in mind that even if someone behaves disrespectfully towards you, it doesn't mean

that you should be disrespectful to them, but you may want to consider a few things.

> *"Pay attention when people react with anger and hostility to your boundaries. You have found the edge of where their respect for you ends"*

If you are in a relationship with a man who behaves disrespectfully towards you, it is worth looking at why you are choosing to be with him. Do you think that you do not deserve better? Are you scared that if you leave him you will not find love again? Do you think that if you give him enough love that he will change? Both men and women can find themselves staying in bad relationships in the hope that their partner will change. By thinking that you can help them to change you are essentially taking responsibility for their bad behaviour. In this way you are not only diminishing yourself, but also allowing them to abdicate responsibility for their choices, which means they are unlikely to face up to the underlying reasons, and so the possibility of change is significantly less likely to happen.

Sometimes, the best way to help someone you care about is to let them go, so that they can find their own path. Of course it is important to be caring and compassionate towards people who have any kind of difficulty in life, but suffering abuse as a result of caring for anyone should never be the price tag. You can be supportive while other people address their own struggles, but do not allow yourself to become their emotional punch bag.

Ultimately, the focus needs to be firmly on you. By ensuring you are strong and independent you give yourself the best opportunity to have healthy relationships, and to set good boundaries. If you can learn to value and respect yourself it is much easier to have a relationship with someone who behaves respectfully towards you.

Respect – just a little bit!

What do you think? Do you think the respect we give to others and the respect we receive from them is a reflection of our self-respect?

48

UNWANTED ATTENTION

"A relationship is only made for two, but some women don't know how to count"

How would you respond if you saw a girl deliberately flirting with your man right in front you?

How about if your man has already made it clear to her that he's not interested – would that make a difference? It is obvious to you that she believes if she persists she can get a response from him, and you can see that she has no intention of modifying her behaviour. You might as well be invisible as far as she is concerned, and it is clear that she is determined to achieve some kind of victory, regardless of the fact that it would be at your expense.

"Trust is earned when actions meet words"

I think in this scenario the best thing to do would be to leave her to it. This doesn't mean that you have to feel alright about her behaviour, you would be well within your rights to feel that she is behaving disrespectfully to both you and to your partner, but if he has set a clear boundary then you know you can trust him and her choices are not going to impact on you in any way, so she can keep chasing her tail if she wants, you know she's not going to get anywhere!

It's fine to express your feelings about her behaviour once you are alone with your partner – in a calm and measured way – after all, he has done nothing to encourage her, so there is no reason to feel upset with him, only with her behaviour.

I'm sure that many of us have found ourselves in situations like this. It can feel humiliating and frustrating, and it can be difficult to know how to react, but by taking a step back and trusting your partner to behave in an adult way you stand the greatest chance of walking away with your dignity in tact. As much as you may want to take control of the situation, it is only likely to cause problems. By staying calm and dispassionate you can comfortably view the situation from the moral high ground and not allow it to get to you.

The important thing in any situation like this is to find ways of dealing with it that bring you closer to your partner, rather than driving a wedge between the two of you. It may even be worth discussing with your partner before you find yourself facing such a scenario exactly what it would mean to you and how it would make you feel. In this way, even if you are staying cool, calm and collected, he won't interpret your detachment as a lack of care about the fact that someone is obviously flirting with you, but rather he will understand that you are simply not allowing her behaviour to have an impact on you.

Unwanted Attention!

Have you experienced something like this? How did you cope? Do you trust your partner to stay in control and handle things or do you feel that he is out of his depth or oblivious to how women behave around him?

49

PURELY PHYSICAL?

"Physical attraction that strong is addictive. And knowing that kind of magic isn't just a fantasy makes me want to find it again. But what about being with someone who makes me a better person? What about sharing my life with someone who adores me as much as I adore him, whom I can always count on, who helps me find my way when I'm lost?

Would you be with a guy who is attracted to you physically but isn't interested in you emotionally or intellectually?

Would you be able to detach yourself emotionally in order to have a purely physical relationship or, if you found yourself falling for him, would you be able to accept that he was only interested in you for your body and not your mind?

I would find it very difficult to be with someone who didn't care about me on a deeper level, because it is important to me to have a partner who admires my inner beauty, not just the way I look. I believe that physical beauty should be an added bonus.

The way we look may be a reflection of who we are to a certain extent, in terms of the clothes we choose, the way we do our hair and make-up, and how we take care of our bodies. It can signal many things about our values, our ambitions, and the way we see ourselves. However, beyond the choices that we make regarding our appearance, the way we look is purely genetic, and it seems strange to attach a sense of worth to something so random. It has little to do with who we are as people. Having a symmetrical face, big eyes or long legs may be considered desirable, but for someone to choose you based purely on these attributes seems to devalue your inner beauty.

> *"It's beautiful when you find someone who is in love with your mind; someone who wants to undress your conscience and make love to your thoughts. Someone who wants to watch you slowly take down all the walls you've built up around your mind and let them inside"*

It's very difficult to maintain a long-term relationship based purely on physical attraction, in part because beauty fades with age, but also because if you do not have any shared interests or beliefs then there will be very little to talk about, beyond superficial conversations about physical attraction. If there is no connection beyond the way you look, it may well leave you feeling lonely, frustrated and undervalued as a person. It may also cause you to invest a great deal of emotional energy in the way you look, which can be a very dangerous road to take, and can lead to massive insecurities.

Let's get physical!

What are your personal experiences of relationships that are centred purely on physical attraction? Are you able to set your emotions to one side in order to have something less involved or have you found yourself getting hurt because men are attracted to you for one thing, and one thing only? Have you ever mistaken a man's physical desire for love?

50

SEPARATE BANK ACCOUNTS

"Money only impresses lazy girls. When a woman works hard, a man with money is a bonus, not a ladder to upgrade"

Do you agree that couples should have separate bank accounts so they can use their own money to buy their own things?

My partner and I have separate bank accounts, and it works very well for us. It allows us to have more autonomy and to make choices about how we spend our money without feeling the need to consult the other person, which allows us a degree of freedom that I feel we may not otherwise have. For example, if I want to buy a dress, a new watch, a handbag or anything else, I'll use my own money to pamper myself, and my man will do the same if he wants to buy cigarettes or wine for his own consumption.

By keeping our finances separate, there are never any disagreements over how much we spend on these items, and that seems like the right thing for us. Provided we contribute an equal share to expenses such as the mortgage and household bills, what we choose to spend the rest of the money that we have worked hard for should really be a matter for us to decide on as individuals.

"Spoil me with loyalty – I can finance myself"

If we are eating out, we will take turns to pay. It makes me feel good to know that we are looking after each other, and to know that I can look after myself, too. I believe that financial independence is one of the keys to feeling confident, and to knowing wholeheartedly that you have true equality in a relationship. Anything that skews the balance in a relationship is potentially going to cause problems, and money is one of the things that is notorious for putting stress onto a relationship.

In addition to this, I think it's only fair to keep finances separate because our men are not our ATM machines, and it is often easier to behave responsibly with money when you have had to work hard for it, rather than dipping into a bigger pot that is made up of both your incomes, when the temptation to spend more than you otherwise might can be far greater!

Clearly, there are circumstances under which it is not possible for both partners to be earning, and in these cases the same criteria do not apply. If you find yourself without an income for any period of time, so that your partner is supporting you, it might be worth having a conversation about whether you can have a designated amount put into a separate account for you to take responsibility for. Needing to go to your partner every time you require money for groceries or other everyday items is certainly not conducive to having a balanced adult relationship. Even if you are not earning, you are still a partnership and it is important that you are able to feel as much a part of the financial side of the partnership as possible.

Separate or joint?

Do you and your partner have separate bank accounts or do you believe that a joint account is the right thing for your relationship?

About the Author

Pearly Tan was born in Malaysia and grew up in a traditional Chinese culture. She immigrated to Australia in 2004 to be with her partner. After successfully overcoming her relationship difficulties, she dedicated herself to helping others facing similar challenges, especially Asian-Western culture relationships.

For all the latest news and views, please visit www.SuccessWithPearly.com to join the mailing list

Share With Pearly

Pearly Tan would love to hear from you. Please visit her website to share your relationship experiences or to leave a comment about this book or on her blog:

www.SuccessWithPearly.com

www.ingramcontent.com/pod-product-compliance
Lightning Source LLC
LaVergne TN
LVHW051602070426
835507LV00021B/2714